Running out of Time

Mark Lankester

Published by Mark Lankester, 2021.

RUNNING OUT OF TIME

First edition. April 12, 2021.

Written by Mark Lankester.

Table of Contents

5

For those who dream

Introduction

'Time is fickle, but faith is a friend.'

Mark Lankester

Destiny is a far-away island, its causeway visible at low tide, straight, flat and wide. Realism is the jagged trail and incoming waves. The defeating of disappointment is true survival and the land obscuring one's goal a mirage. Yesterday is blurred, but tomorrow is a blank canvas. I have no answers to the bigger question, but say yes to fresh adventures.

Footnotes in history, and distant memories of match days watching Ipswich Town FC on the terraces, at 45 years young I drafted several short stories I have since discarded. Albeit, faded rose-tinted snap shots survive recalled within these pages, for technicoloured dreams burnt a vibrant glow, recalling Arnie Muhren, Thijssen, Beattie and Co.

One eye on the future and the other in the past, I wanted to write of the positives of a run, but somewhat distracted, I sought to reclaim fading youth. The wave of depression, a test of faith, the book put on ice; I entered yet another marathon, and when one stumbled, the story appeared in a haze, urging me to get up off the ropes and fight.

Nine months before the Big Five-O, I wrote once more. This is a glimpse back, sign posting the significant events and cultural changes experienced. I tell of childhood, adolescence, and the conflict in aging. The green fields of home in Suffolk, England feature throughout, and often frame my fears and doubt.

Withal, I include the marathons and various races run within 26.2 chapters, as an analogy on a route towards half a century. The initial miles a breeze, others were rocky under foot, and the wall unexpected. A line a day, a page a week, sleepless nights and words to tweak, I often gazed upon high and asked the question why. The answer is a simple kindness. No thunder and lightning required.

The metaphor hides emotion. For many men consider it a weakness to drop their guard and admit to the struggle. Modern society wants them to open their heart nowadays, yet when I was growing up society frowned upon and ridiculed such things. Man up, and stiff upper lips sucking in a distant stare in silence, I scribe innermost thoughts on paper and march on forth, for if I speak, you think me weak.

Sport bridges a cultural divide, and whilst out training in Lake Garda I met a Sicilian weaving the hilly terrain. Germany had just beaten Italy in Euro 2016, and more expressive than Brits are as a nation I called for no translator to explain his sorrow. Stefano's comment 'amo correre' to one's untrained ear mirrored 'I'm a cool runner'. I thought him vain. Ignorance divides, not language, culture, and religion.

In the sunshine, as we ran up the steep slopes, we needed only a knowing glance, and when we could climb no higher, we watched the sun appear on the horizon. For a splendido scenario, I understood to perfection, early morning sunrise remarkable, whether it shines on Limone sul Garda or Salthouse Harbour.

No matter how tough times become, a sunnier day awaits. Age was a tenacious adversary. Today the foe is a friend, because without maturity, I misread the text. The cusp of older and a road travelled, challenges are there to conquer. On a voyage of self-discovery, angst still raged penning these tales, but in part writing helped me turn a corner and find a guiding light.

The greatest test of endurance I have undertook required no shoes, only patience and hours burning the midnight oil, and four years on if you read these words, it was worth every minute. Nothing worthwhile is easy, for if it were we would never see life's wonder. Trust a storm my readers and ride on through, because in this mortal coil it is the best you can   do.

Passing the Baton

Mile 1

'Change is inevitable. Change is constant.'

Benjamin Disraeli

I ran my first London Marathon in 1999, and although an awe-inspiring experience, I knew one could run faster. For, on April 23rd 2006, at the age of 38, I confronted the monster once more, a fitter and stronger soul to finish just shy of three and a half hours. Surreal, as if floating in another body, I have never surpassed those heights since.

Today I can interpret that period with the benefit of hindsight, as if stepping back to view the beauty of a painting. Father Time creeps up on every mortal, and few elite athletes continue past the age of 40. The metabolism slows, and the body takes longer to recover. More rest days equals less training. Fitness is harder to keep and diet is vital.

You may think you are in better shape than when younger, and while this might be true, you probably train more and lead a healthier lifestyle.

The human frame is sharper and more resilient in youth. Brian Clough once argued that there was nothing we could do better physically after our thirties. He was right to an extent, but Stanley Matthews played football until he was 50. That said, he had the edge running on Blackpool Beach, his diet and foresight light years ahead of peers.

Rockers such as Mick Jagger have not let age define them, and Sylvester Stallone continues to make action movies. We can still set targets and goals when not at our peak. Floating like a rudderless ship, I never understood the philosophy during my mid-forties. Nor did I want to talk the talk, long after the boat had sailed.

The descent is swift, without a positive perspective and a healthy lifestyle. I used to think at the top of a mountain that I could go no higher. Howbeit, today, as I write, I see the world from a different viewpoint, for when the arm is strong, reach for the stars.

Muhammad Ali once yelled he was still the greatest. He may well have been, but he too carried on past his prime. I guess he wanted to be the 'champ' at 40. More than a boxer, he transcended the sport, and his refusal to serve in the army during the Vietnam War resulted in a three-year ban from boxing. People thought the icon finished, but in defiance, he returned from the wilderness to face Joe Fraser.

In 1974, in the fight known as the 'Rumble in the Jungle', he fought a younger foe the critics considered invincible. Yet he achieved the impossible, and my God, in the words of Harry Carpenter the famous commentator, he really did reclaim the title at the age of 32!

Ali should have finished on top, but faded after too many fights, his health suffering. Larry Holmes cried after he beat his hero, and one month before his 40th birthday, he lost again against Trevor Berbick. He admitted, father time had caught up and retired. Nobody defeats nature's clock, but he inspired millions in and out of the ring, sowing the seeds of self-belief.

Fear of failure is an Everest to climb, a rhyme that pulls us back one-step at a time. A Viking in 800 AD would most likely be a grandfather and dead by middle age. If he had not died in battle or of disease, his son would have succeeded him. As with two stags locking horns, in nature conflict occurs.

The baton has to pass forward to the next generation, so our genes survive and thrive. I clashed with my dad when I was 20. We fought for territory, tripped over each other on shift work and invaded each other's space. I left home at 21. It was the natural order.

The Scandinavian warriors believed in Valhalla, the hall of the slain warrior, convinced if they perished in war they would live eternally. The elderly were rare in those times. Most of the Norse men did not strive to reclaim their youth. They never had the chance.

People's life expectancy is longer now. The most ferocious competitors at races are well over 40! I resolved not to let my younger self-go without a fight, and it was a tough, rocky road of discovery.

George Foreman a man crushed after the defeat against Ali had a spiritual awakening years later. Two decades after he lost his crown, determined to show older was not a death sentence, he regained the global title a few days short of his 46th birthday.

In 2013, across the pond in England, a young pretender would have issued a challenge if I had been an ancient Viking. Therefore, with that in mind, I set a self-afflicted goal.

Shortly before my son turned 18, I decided to pass on the proverbial baton. He had trained with me throughout his teens and had recently humbled his father in several middle-distance races. I wished I were younger. However, a few months on fitness had improved when we both entered the Stowmarket Striders Scenic 7, a local seven-mile road race held on Remembrance Sunday.

November 11th was a typical British crisp winter morning, and up for the test, I prepared to roll back the years. My lad had done the distance in training, but it was his first competitively and I knew he would go off too fast. A decade before, at the same venue, I scampered round the course in 47:33. I would have to match that time to finish ahead, and I knew it would be an unquestionable challenge.

The race started at 11:02 am, after we stood for a two-minute silence for those soldiers who fought and died to protect our way of life. During this time, I thought of Grandad and the stories he told me of the Second World War, sanitised tales to a young boy, not the genuine horror. Sadly, I only remember a few, of which I will now share...

Once, he was sitting in an open truck with his friends looking back on the road, when a vehicle drew up behind them. As he recalled the tale, he mimicked the panicked expression on the German driver's face as he realised what was unfolding. Swiftly he veered off in another direction, much to the relief of both parties I am sure.

Another time lost on patrol in woodland able to locate his regiment, he walked a while before detecting a light in the distance. Luckily, he had been wandering in circles, but on nearing the glow, he knew not whether it was friend or foe.

He enjoyed a pint, as many of us do, and while relaxing, drank a beer, not realising a wasp was wading in the glass. Thankfully, he suffered no ill effects. Whilst recalling those stories, I cannot help visualising the black and white film 'Ice Cold in Alex'. In the classic Second World War tale, four characters struggled across a desert in Egypt to get to British lines, and once there, enjoyed a lager in a local bar.

I picture Grandad in that scene. He died when I was young, and I wish I could remember more tales. He served in the Eighth Army, fought in Tobruk, and saw his best friend killed. Every soul has a story to share. Although as generations pass, most vanish through the winds of time.

Carlsberg used a clip of the old flick for a commercial many years later. John Mills, who starred, grew up in Felixstowe, a few miles from my home in Ipswich where a theatre bears his name. Younger generations might be more familiar with his grandson Crispian from the rock band Kula Shaker.

My great grandmother lost her husband in the First World War. She married again and gave birth to my dad's father. Recently, my parents found out his name and visited the memorial. The paradox is that if he had survived, I would not exist. I feel connected to the poor lad who never lived to have a family, and I am forever mindful of fates power to change everything.

One minute passed slowly, as I stood lost in thought. The wind whipped across the flat landscape and I regretted wearing a vest. Edward Norton Lorenz studied weather patterns and coined the phrase 'butterfly effect'. He suggested that the flap of the insect's wings might set off a huge chain of events, such as a distant storm.

Every action, however small, can shift our destiny. The insect, originally a 'flutterby', is merely an Englishman's mispronunciation that has stuck for perpetuity. Perhaps he was Suffolk born, because we do talk in rhyme. Ali floated like the proverbial, yet stung as if a bee, the legacy for all to see.

Boom, its 2013, and claps and cheers ring out to break the silence, bringing me out of the daydream. On the walk to the start, just before the outset, I wished my lad luck, and when the claxon blew, he left me stranded. However, within two miles, I closed the gap. I had watched Rocky III days earlier. The movies inspired, and a quote from the blockbuster jumped into my brain – 'go for it!'...

Although I eventually overtook doubt had set in by mile four, but with a stern gaze, I refused to turn my head. It was possible to run 7:30 pace for another 20 minutes, despite a nagging doubt I was older, and with two miles left, I focused and confidence rose.

Suddenly, a woman I knew cycled by giving much needed encouragement to weary runners and told me my lad was close. Glad he was okay, no way could I move faster and when a pal drew up on his bike to repeat the message, retirement from running and taking up cycling seemed a viable option.

To be brutally honest, by 10k, I could not have given a four-ex, but sure could have done with a pint. The Castlemaine brand of beer, popularised in an Australian commercial, disappeared from the shelves in England for a time. Thankfully, it has since returned for the retro market. There is always a place for nostalgia.

Near the Stowmarket Leisure Centre, the finish loomed as I braced myself for one last effort. Breath heavy, I ached from head to toe and considered taking my foot off the gas. Just as I sucked air in to strengthen myself for the final 150 metres, a giant shadow appeared on the ground. It was my boy, and in a sprint to the line and blinded by the light, I finished ahead by a second.

A pal told my son he had left it too late to close the gap. I am sure if it had been 100 metres further, he would have done so. He just ran out of road. Experience helps. Afterwards, I was emotional, not because of the battle, but because he was growing stronger and I older. Metaphorically, at 45, I had had a good run. There are moments when you realise your own story is being written while it plays out. One of those was a chilly November morning in Stowmarket.

A few weeks later, I drove my daughter and friends into town for their first visit to a nightclub. On the journey home, I watched young people heading out for the night. It did not seem long ago I was clubbing myself. Time waits for no man. For a few years, I sought to reclaim lost youth. Sometimes I had fun and other times it was tragic.

Old age sneaks up while we worry over the future and before we know it, here we are. John Lennon once declared that life happens while making other plans. He reflected on a conflict we all share when he said those words. Imagine if you returned in time and corrected those mistakes. Destiny is an intricate maze, one slight turn and our destination changes. We can do nothing to alter history; it has created who we are today.

When I read stories or watch them on TV, I notice how the narrative rushes through a characters' childhood until the adult tale arrives. Early years are a foundation, significant in establishing identity. Elvis picked up a guitar as a child and learnt to sing, never knowing what the future would bring. I looked to the heavens for inspiration as a boy. Half a century has passed and I still share those dreams.

Yesterday, adulthood was far away, but those times mean more than words can say. The Internet has changed our world. We are now closer together, yet further apart. Ergo, as I tell this tale in a Suffolk voice, I must first rewind the clock back to those hazy days of innocence. Once upon a time, long ago in a rural town called Ipswich...

Yesterday

Mile 2

'I ran home as fast as I could, breathless and in wonderment, the sun and the moon both glittering in the afternoon sky, eclipsed by rainfall as if a tear from David Bowie's eye.'

Mark Lankester

Born on Easter Sunday, April 14th 1968, within a mile of my local football club's stadium, Cliff Richard sang congratulations from radios throughout Britain. A few miles away in Thetford, the BBC began shooting the first episode of the wartime comedy Dad's Army.

Grandad was a lifelong Manchester United supporter from Lancashire, and 24 hours earlier, Best and Charlton had both scored at Old Trafford. They were to be European Champions by the summer. Ipswich, our little town were soon to join them in the top flight. The Beatles were all together now in a Yellow Submarine, and their music company Apple Corps boldly went global.

Meanwhile, as Lennon sang of revolution, two runners stood on an Olympic podium, with black-gloved hands aloft in defiance. Peter Norman, the

Australian in the foreground of the iconic photo, did not raise a fist. Instead, took a literal and metaphorical stand by wearing a human rights badge in solidarity.

I wondered who the white lad was, sometimes erased from the image. His career slid like a rolling stone in the aftermath. Tommie Smith and John Carlos the men he supported were poll bearers at his funeral. Memories fade, but a picture paints a thousand words. Running seemed the noble sport as old as life itself, one man versus another, undivided by creed, class and religion.

Whilst I learnt to walk, three American astronauts landed on the Moon, a giant leap for humankind. Two men Neil Armstrong and Buzz Aldrin walked the surface, while a third snapped a photo of every living being on the Earth, including his friends. The photographer Michael Collins was the only Earthling not to appear in the picture.

Today he could have taken a selfie, with the world and his colleagues in the backdrop. How wonderful would that have been! Histories forgotten hero, and throughout this book I recall a few. I have to thank the Spacemen for the TV series, 'The Clangers' which may never have existed without them.

David Bowie released 'Space Oddity' in 1969 and the era I know and remember materialised. In times that are more recent, a television saga adopted his song 'Life on Mars' as its soundtrack and title. The show struck a chord. The protagonist was the same age as I and time travelled from the present to 1973. When he arrived, he saw himself as a small child. Whilst the opening credits rang out, childhood memories came flooding back. I began school Easter that year.

Nursery was a conservatory at Mrs Jones's house. There were about a dozen of us at preschool and I loved it. During the summer, we played on a climbing frame and in a sandpit. Her son, who was about 18 brought along his guitar. He performed various songs about Vera, Chuck, Dave, Jude, Desmond, and Eleanor Rigby. He looked a little like David Cassidy. At the time I was unaware most were Beatle tunes. In a town where I was born he sang of getting old and losing his hair, but he made a sad song sound better and shouted yeah, yeah. Today he would be about 64. I wonder what happened to that lad. Perhaps he is mending a fuse, or doing the garden in a cottage somewhere in the Isle of Wight.

Andy Warhol, the eminent artist once declared all of us would have 15 minutes of fame. Mine arrived two days before my fifth birthday. Mum had dressed me up smart to go on an adventure. Dad drove a red Herbie car, and strangely, the boot was at the front of the vehicle. After for what seemed forever, we showed up in a far-off land called Norwich. When we got there and parked, I glanced up at an enormous building. The architecture was Victorian in appearance, nothing unique in the seventies. Above the door was a gigantic gold sign that read Anglia Television. Once inside, we sat in a lobby full of other infants and parents.

Romper Room was the TV extravaganza I was about to appear on. I believed I had started a new preschool, the premise similar. We played games and sang songs, and I spoke to a lad named Sam. The only part that was odd was the big cameras on tripods. The men peering through the lenses intrigued as I wandercd up to them. Mrs Rosalyn our teacher asked us if we had been good doobies, while lifting what resembled a tennis racket to her face. Before we left, she gave me a certificate and a doobie toy to take home. Crying, I was sure I had been naughty for walking up to the camera operators.

When Anglia broadcast the show, family and friends came round to watch. Before I appeared on the goggle box, a Silver Knight on Horseback turned nonchalantly on a plate to the short segment of music by the composer Handel. Never did I see a rerun. I could write to producers and enquire if they have a copy. This is improbable. If the rival station the BBC were wiping Dad's Army classics, I doubt an ancient episode survives in Norwich.

In those days, my world tiny, a walk to the nearby shops and park was an adventure. We lived on a main road and I never ventured out without an adult. Heavy trucks rolled through the neighbourhood daily. A decade later, they built the Orwell Bridge to free up traffic in the town.

Once I saw a bus zoom past with smashed windows, and I asked Mum why it did not stop. She said it was because it had a broken window. Words I took literally, thus having an image of the poor bloke driving in circles, until he ran out of petrol.

Double-decker buses had no doors, and we jumped on to seize a metal pole. Attempting to climb the stairs as the driver pulled away precarious. Health and safety did not exist. Builders rarely wore hard hats and I recall John Noakes climbing Nelson Column with no harness. The pigeons must have thought him mad. Mum and Dad switched off everything electrical before bed. In those periods, it was common for televisions to overheat and set fire to the curtains.

Heavy industry still prevailed, in a symphonic sound of machinery and crashing of steel. Manufacturers made cars with heavier metal than today, and doors slammed with a crunch. Manual work was tougher, binmen carried hefty bins and someone was always on strike. Prime Minister Ted Heath never appeared happy. I could not fathom why he had not retired, because Grandad looked younger.

Posties and a host of working men sported black donkey jackets, people whistled and a few office workers still wore Mr Benn bowler hats. Those days are grimy even through rose-tinted glasses. Often I heard folk moan about the state of the country. For, politicians appeared to be responsible for everything bad. Sometimes the lights would go out in the house, and Mum would scurry about searching for candles. Excited, I imagined a bloke from the government turning them off with a giant switch.

Mum made bread when there was a baker's strike. The smell I loved and ate some dough before she placed the tray in the oven, white powder covering hands. Long hair prevailed, and perhaps the barbershops were in dispute with customers. Thick smoke bellowed from Victorian chimneys, and the past really seems like another universe. My parents were young and enjoyed music, so the wireless was on regularly.

Bowie and Bolan boomed from a distant world. Glam rock and beautiful ballads evoked an era of optimism for the future. Was there life on Mars, would this 20th century boy visit one day? Occasionally, a less glamorous tune would emanate from the airways, such as some bloke shouting mouldy old dough. Maybe the singer was a worker from a bakery making a record in his spare time!

Brian Cant, born in Ipswich, a hero presented Play School and narrated Chigley and Trumpton. Those halcyon days of bliss and misunderstandings, the theme tune to 'Crossroads' made me sad, so too the Gilbert O'Sullivan ballad about Claire. Holidays were a thrill, bucket and spade gathered in exited anticipation; we could fly to Butlin's mega quick on Concorde faster than the speed of light!

Those preschool memories are hazy. I remember little about the interior of the home we once lived. However, the garden was spacious and backed onto an allotment. The open landscape appeared wild and untamed. My first pet was a rabbit who we christened Brownie because he was brown. I say he, it may have been a girl.

My long-eared friend escaped soon after by chewing through the wire mesh of his hutch. Because of the dark, I hoped he found carrots to keep him going on his adventure. I knew rabbits liked them because Bugs Bunny ate the orange veg all the time. He was probably happier free. Yet I prayed Elmer Fudd would not catch him, cos he hated wabbits.

Our elderly neighbours had a low wooden fence I often clambered to grab their attention. The old dear would come out with a handful of cornflakes. Although not hungry, I considered it a game. The other side lived an Alsatian dog I avoided at all costs.

Once, I locked my mum out of the kitchen by slipping the bolt on the door. She had to clamber through a window. I am unsure this is a true memory, perhaps I heard my parents talk of it. Not only did I like Kellogg's cereals, I thought nothing of eating soil, sand, and tarmac. Hell, I survived!

Early childhood recollections before the age of five are a mixture of fuzzy images. Facts I have checked with older relatives. A faint memory could be my auntie giving me sweets instead of a grandma. Little details I get wrong sometimes.

Now, if my children want to remember younger days, they can watch one of my homemade videos. I have a distant recollection of a holiday in Rockley Sands. I call to mind playing crazy golf, my grandparents visiting and Dad having a Volkswagen Beetle car. Rural Suffolk and quintessential English eccentrics set the backdrop to my formative years.

Old money a confusing currency, I remember 'pounds, shillings, pence', and adults using phrases such as 'two and six', but I never figured out what it meant. Decimalisation arrived on the 15th of February 1971. The outdated tender circulated for a while after that date. Once whilst in Woolworths, my great-grandmother placed a 'thrupenny-bit' in my palm. The 12-sided coin I gave to a woman at the till, and as if by magic, sweets appeared in a tiny bag.

During a nostalgia TV series recently, guests talked fondly of shows from their childhood. These personalities were younger than I was, and remembered 'Here Comes the Double Deckers!' with perfect recall, for me a blurred memory in every sense. Two details I conjure up were children playing on a bus and a distinct lad with glasses.

One day when the show was on, in my excitement, while running about I banged my head against the wall. Mum ran into the room. I was crying and could not see. She told me not to be daft and settled me on the sofa. The programme was a blur apart from red dots jumping about the screen. Yep, I should have gone to hospital. Yet, this was the seventies, and my sight returned that evening.

Older people used to say policemen were getting younger. Now they resemble extras from a futuristic movie. I still expect to see them wearing those custodian helmets. Jack Warner in the popular TV series 'Dixon of Dock Green' wore one. Heck, he was an elderly bobby to be roaming the beat. However, he looked spritely considering Dirk Bogarde shot him dead 25 years beforehand. The old boy stood outside the station after every episode and told us not to worry, bidding everybody goodnight. Nice man and I felt safe he was out there catching criminals.

The past is so familiar, and the present sometimes strange as if in a dream. Donald Trump is President of the United States. Mark, go back to sleep. When we remember something, we do not recall the actual event, but the last occasion we thought of it. When a song comes on the radio, it transports me to a moment in time. As I relive many things, it will become a memory of me typing this story. Life memories and places are reflective looking glasses.

Speaking of which when I was a kid wandering around the town centre one morning with Mum, we walked into a store called John Menzies. We strode up to the top floor. Mirrors were both sides of us on the staircase. Our reflections repeated themselves into the distance. This mesmerised me as I could see myself getting smaller and smaller.

Often I will be somewhere that prompts an echo. While walking on the promenade in Felixstowe yesterday, the song 'Tiger feet' splashed across my mind as if a giant wave from the shore. The picture accompanying the tune was much later. In the late eighties with teenage friends, we were in the arcade on the sea front while the seventies classic played. Pals commented on how naff and dated the music sounded. I have lived in Ipswich for 50 years and every corner of most streets spits out sounds and ghosts of long ago.

Christchurch Park, I visit often, a constant in my life. When I was a boy, I fed the ducks and heard a distant roar. I asked my parents what it was. The noise was the supporters at Portman Road football ground. Ipswich Town FC was on the cusp of greatness under Bobby Robson. For now, my existence was nursery rhymes, fuzzy felt, and plasticine. However, I had heard of George Best. His name was a bit of a riddle, best at what, a little like who is on first base whose on second. Grandad was upset, because Bestie had ran away. Perhaps it was because of the cold. Supporters always wore scarfs. Stadiums must have been freezing!

A Tudor Mansion stands within the grounds, a spooky dwelling as a child. I thought they should build a new one. Ironic thoughts of childhood, over the last 40 years many buildings have disappeared from Suffolk, some built in my lifetime. We walked past Sir Alf Ramsey's house on the way home. Alfie won us the World Cup, so very impressed with our little town I was.

Gran told me there was once a bandstand in the park, before Teddy Boys burnt it to the ground. The phrase was a blanket term she used to describe delinquent teenagers. There was a revival in the early seventies. They strutted about like peacocks, in their bright coloured socks. Their dress sense fascinated me when small.

Everywhere I looked, there were billboards and hoardings on bridges, stores and street corners advertising cigarettes. More people smoked back then. Cafeterias smelt of smoke and older folk just left unlit cigs hang from their mouths. Not the best look. Old men wore a shirt and tie when retired, and tattoos were rare unless you crossed paths with a pirate!

I spent many happy times round my grandparents with my younger sister. Prefabs sprouted up all over the country after the Second World War, most are now private and sort after properties. I still drive past that little bungalow remembering the garden and the smell of stew and dumplings. No one has since cooked them the same, a real shame. Today I picture Brooke Bond tea cards, a coal fire and an array of memorabilia. Although a bygone time, I will never forget.

Life changed forever, when Mum called upstairs to tell me I was to start school the next day. Mama, I'm crazy now, come up and see me smile. Welcome, the Young Americans, glam rock hits, happy days and all the Young Dudes. See my go-kart jive, in Bachman-Turner Overdrive. Wig-Wam Bam, walk on the wild side children of the revolution. Goodbye to Jane, let us introduce the angel faced Jenny, and the arch villain   Mr   Spitfire.

Spitfire

Mile 3

'I feared walls, fools and language, three crosses to bear, adulthood a salvation.'

Mark Lankester

I arrived first day at school confident, after the televised fame of Romper Room. Mum walked me the 10-minute journey. To one's horror, I soon realised it was for keeps. Built in the sixties, the building modern, children born before Christmas started earlier than I and had been inmates for months, readily regimented in subservience.

Pray for your sins and sing a hymn, and then learning would begin in Ernest, whoever he may be, and they said our country ruled land and sea. A good memory, a handy tool, if only a fool speaks parrot fashion echoed to the adult word, for he is right your free hand wrong.

Day one, a lad with a large Mr Man plaster on his nose introduced himself. Apparently, he had used the subterfuge to bunk off lessons. It cut no ice with the teacher, who inspected his non-existent injury. However, in a stroke of superb man management, she had allowed him to keep the protective dressing. He

30

must have had a box full of plasters handy, for the much-loved Arthur Lowe voiced characters shared upon his beak changed in a hurry, whether it be Topsy-Turvy, Forgetful or Worry.

Alan and I hit it off as we both liked the books and cartoons, and six months older, he took me under his wing. I should have nicknamed him Mister Nosey, but few infants have a one-liner of that calibre. Although he repeatedly got into fights, he left me alone. Within a few weeks, things changed in a dispute over a game of marbles. Poked in the eye I did cry, and the experience set me up for the jungle outside of a teacher's world.

A round dome resembling the Moon stood magnificently in the playground, painted grey over a tar like material, good to pick with fingernails and chew. Inside the futuristic structure, there was a swimming pool. With the right foot rooted to the floor, I became quite proficient at breaststroke. Covered in talc to get dry, in hindsight, a towel would have been easier. The chlorine made the eyes sting, and I assumed that Alan peeing in the deep end had caused the irritation.

Margaret Thatcher, the 'milk snatcher' pinched our free morning drinks that smelt with a yellow goo on the bottled rim. The song children sang of her reminded me of the evil Child Catcher character from a classic children's film. Childhood memories are powerful. Some claim the Iron Lady regretted the decision all those years ago. Kiddies grow up and vote, but nae bothered, I preferred coke.

Annual summer sports day should have been fun, but I stumbled on a fool with a spoon, legs debilitated within a sack with parents watching. Instead, I would have willingly done the proper run and finished last in unathletic dreaded shame.

The event everybody watched with anticipation was the mum's 100-metre sprint. Most wore jeans or skirts and inappropriate shoes and joined on a whim. Withal, one mature woman stood out, wearing athletic clothing. Perhaps a competitive runner, she won by a canter every year and celebrated as if winning the Olympics.

On this day, as she warmed up, others chatted nonchalantly, unperturbed. When the contest began, once again within seconds, she pulled away with arms raised victoriously. The start gun and celebration instantaneous, she stumbled.

Shocked and somewhat embarrassed, a girl in flared trousers ran past to win, with a radiant smile in a waddle of style. Cheers for the result louder than customary boys chanted 'she fell over', and though I did the same, I felt an innermost shame when she cried. For I felt her pain knowing perhaps the aging Queen of the track had her own finale planned.

A sickly child, once I had my tonsils removed. The operation cancelled frequently, because of other illnesses, the ward a revolving door, I soon dropped behind in lessons. The hospital Victorian in style and ambience became a classroom of kinship with friendships fleeting. Meals were not as nice as at home, and the bacon greasy. Natheless, the nurses were angels.

Whenever I see an episode of The Royal, I cannot help but think of those times. The nostalgic drama was a spinoff from the beloved TV show Heartbeat, which never moved past 1969 even though it ran for 18 years. That is a shame, the cultural events a treasure trove to draw on in the decades that followed. Imagine if I had been born in the fictional Aidenfield. I would have stayed a toddler for quite a while.

The scary storybook Rumpelstiltskin spawned oh so many nightmares, and television programmes were often creepy. When I was a tad older, the movie Jaws terrified. Today, whenever I swim in the sea, I recall the black fin above the water and haunting soundtrack enough to instil the dread that applied to the classroom.

In 1975, I was seven, and we nicknamed our teacher Mr Spitfire as he circled ready to bite. From the start, I sat near the front of the class, and whether he knew of my missed schooling, I cannot be certain.

Bullies home in on easy prey. Nature the survival of the fittest, they ostracise the weakest, and the metaphorical shark had me in his sights, my desk close and handy. Sporting an unkempt beard, he looked 40, but could have been far younger. He had issues with my writing style: and posh and strict he spat when he spoke, hence the name. If unlucky, a piece of phlegm flew in one's eye. If I upset him, I got a ruler across my hand, sometimes on the backside - narrow side on for greatest effect.

Once he ordered a prefect to inform him if anybody spoke in his absence. A recipe for disaster, this trustworthy pupil of the same age as peers enforced discipline when teachers were not around. When he disappeared, my friend Dave whispered of the footballing heroics of Kevin Beattie, who had scored a pearler from the halfway line against the Mighty Leeds. Painfully as was, I told him to be quiet, fearing the adult wrath of a wooden ruler.

Beardy locks returned and inquired if anyone had spoken. The nark spilled the beans in a flash, and spitting mad he whacked us both hard on the posterior. My mate refused to show it hurt, so united in defiance I did the same. Because of this, he slapped again, harder. I wrote left-handed, and forced to use the right, if I failed another whacking rained on from high, the reason I do not know why.

Another incident occurred with the same friend while eating lunch in the hall. A dinner lady called out to ask if anyone wanted more chocolate crunch, a desert I adored. Yet in a Oliver Twist when I went to collect more, Dave seized my arm and ordered me to stay, as he was yet to finish and when he pulled, my sleeve became twice as long.

In a flash, Spitfire grabbed our ears. While repairing a piano, he had seen everything, and in a fit of anger belted our butts with a pair of pliers. I noticed he had sweat patches under his arms and smelt, and guessed he was trying to impress the very attractive teaching assistant with his macho antics. When our bearded nemesis stormed off, she asked if we were okay.

The young woman resembled Jenny Agutter from the Railway Children film. I liked her but was not sure why I had those thoughts. We tried to look composed, as to cry in her presence an embarrassment. I hoped to be in her class and wondered if she appreciated maps. Frank from another year said he developed a stutter when she talked to him. If I saw her walking towards me in the corridor, my breathing went funny and I stared at the floor. We were still far too immature to understand those emotions.

Throughout the era, I collected football sticker albums. The stats fascinated, and the data rose from the pages as if in the voice of John Motson. Packs of them, we swapped at break-time, with an Ipswich Town player, a valuable currency, with mates giving up several less important stars in exchange. Kevin Beattie a sought after hero, Dad spoke of him in much the same way he did George Best. Keegan was a superstar, and his Liverpool team would dominate the seventies and beyond. Red scarfs popped up all over Suffolk like daffodils, for everybody loves a winner. Local glory comes to those who wait patience a virtue.

Parents' evening loomed at the end of term. For days, I prayed for divine intervention. Before the visit, Spitfire held a geography lesson that morning. In a stroke of luck, inside my World Cup sticker album, a map showed what country each team came from, and when he pointed to distant countries, my left arm shot up, knowing most. That night he told Mum and Dad I had had a red-letter day, whatever that meant. Though never considering myself clever, I was not stupid. Why hold a pencil in the wrong hand.

Once, our teacher asked everyone whom they thought most likely to write a book when an adult. To my amazement, most suggested yours truly. Somewhat stunned, he requested the reasons. Tony said I enjoyed telling stories, and the prefect mentioned I doodled whilst staring out of the window during Maths. Yep, more than a few were enjoying my discomfort, but the fire of phlegm listened with interest and nodded in my direction, as if to say listen and learn. As I now sit here writing, I realise I was an immense disappointment.

The next morning, the author of the Bobby Brewster books visited. The stories were popular with youngsters. Plots involved objects coming to life in the young boy's house. Mr Todd stood on stage and challenged us to think up a short tale to send to him in a competition. If he thought an essay good, he would use it as an inspiration for a book. Months afterwards, once again, we congregated in the assembly hall. The writer read out the winners and I was amongst the names.

I vowed that when a man I would confront Spitfire, and three decades later, I passed him in the street. Yet, he was grey and much older and I felt no animosity. The tales I told you are not unique, and I am disturbed that back in the day nobody challenged that behaviour. Have you ever heard the phrase 'It never did me any harm'? Feared him I did, but never respected.

Perhaps he went to a public school, had a torrid experience, and then ventured into adulthood full of anger. He might have deemed himself a failure when he landed with Suffolk's finest, for we should encourage children to debate and question.

Jessica, a classroom friend, sat to my left, our elbows knocking. For pencil in hand I knew not Shakespeare invented her name, a poetic of historic fame who gave a word nuance and a language to reclaim. Olivia, another, I pass on forth in my footsteps an English Rose christened.

I may have figured out why I had difficulties with English. Words I wrote as they sounded. Most of my family going back generations came from Ipswich. I have a strong Suffolk dialect, as do many local people.

Locals pronounce 'picture' as 'pitcher' and shopping as 'sharpin'. To an untrained ear, it often sounds as if we are asking a question as a sentence ends. As an adult, I hid my accent when attending job interviews or in formal settings. I no longer do this, so proud am I of home a land of wonder its coastline 50 mile, its football team once so full of guile.

Boys larking about in Ipswich, we were appalled at local accents and phrases, the farmer tone, not our own. As lads, we never thought we talked the rhyme, but in reality, we were the same. How wuz oi spuz t'now, the Queens English was play'in silly buggers.

I spent a lot of time at my friend's house. He had two brothers, so I did not add to the mayhem. His dad was a lovely bloke who always tried to join in with the banter. We laughed at his expressions, such as, 'I will woe betide you'. Never did I bother inquiring what it meant, although it sounded ridiculous.

On a Sunday evening, the theme tune to Black Beauty emanated from the TV, as I worried of spelling tests on the Monday. A magnificent horse appeared on the screen, running free through the countryside. Sadness overwhelmed and I craved the freedom of the school summer hols. I am certain I had periods of depression, but cannot be sure if the cause was nature, nurture or environment. Okay, life was good, but you would have to wear a giant set of rose-tinted glasses to say it was bliss.

In 1976, it was the hottest summer since records began. Felixstowe is a 20-minute drive, or a 10-mile run from home. We spent many a weekend there, never far from the pier. On hot days, we waded in the ocean and lay behind windbreakers, as often blustery on the coast. People flocked to the seaside and swam with no fear of pollution. Foreign holidays were not common. Beach huts were popular, and families enjoyed a cup of tea in their palace by the sea.

Retired folk walked the promenade with hankies on heads, and the only occasion some of them had travelled overseas was during the war. Times changed, but the seventies were simpler days. I recall walking to the hydrant to fill up buckets when authorities imposed a hosepipe ban. We tipped bath water on the garden as not to waste. If some ignored the policy, lush green lawns were few.

The grown-ups sunbathed, as they considered it healthy. With no looking glass into the future, I became bored lying in the sun. I pestered my parents for money to go to the arcade on the pier. This was before Space Invaders, Donkey Kong and Pac-Man. When I ran out of money, I returned to ask for ice cream.

Although I learnt no sharks lurked in Felixstowe, I feared Jaws might get lost and hungry. Never have I let that fear go. Once, after plucking up the courage to tiptoe into the waves, I trod on something. The pain was as if I had put my foot in a bucket of glass. Arghh, jellyfish, and I screamed blue murder!

On another occasion, Mum sat on a piece of chewing gum and ranted for ages how dreadful it was that yobs littered the beach. Recently, I reminded them of this story. Dad admitted he was the guilty party, and I cannot blame him for keeping quiet.

There used to be a store in Felixstowe called The Old Owl Art Shop, and once some joker painted an F in front of the words owl and art. I have qualms it was rockers, for they were too busy combing their quiffs.

Around that period, I noticed teenagers with spikey hair and a few were girls. I doubt they sunbathed with those complexions. However, they were patriotic and celebrated the Queen by wearing the Union Jack. Poor as church mice, they mended their clothes with safety pins.

I wondered what fashion trend I would adopt when I grew up. A fool such as I, and all shook up, I was to discover a king from a foreign land, and a fear of barbershops. Welcome to my world and follow that dream, readers. For if, reality is childhood wonder, adulthood apathy destroys ones vision, mortals journey brief.

The King and I

....
....

Mile 4

'The past is a foreign country; they do things
differently there.'

L.P Hartley

Mile 4 is early in a marathon. Unless you have any serious underling issues, you are warming up with no knowledge of what awaits. When I was nine years old, major upsets were none and the road to maturity had no map, and the metaphorical smiles that followed signposted the way to adulthood. Yet only having known Suffolk and the people I met, my worldview was taking shape. The only insight I had of far-off lands was through the medium of TV and film, and much of it was American repeats of a bygone generation.

In 1977, I was not fully aware of rock music. There were songs I appreciated, but I was oblivious to who sang them and more interested in the serious currency of marbles. Punk I had noticed, but seldom heard their tunes on the radio. The starling dudes looked peculiar in the age of flared trousers. A teenybopper in our locality called Jim resembled a member of the Bay City Rollers, a successful boy band of the era.

Then, suddenly, he changed his image by sporting a spikey hairdo and ripped jeans.

June 7th was the Silver Jubilee, and we celebrated 25 years of Elizabeth II at the throne with street parties throughout the country. There was one where we lived. Neighbours made food, and my sister and I entered a fancy dress competition. Mum dressed me as Batman, and Jimmy hovered on the periphery in his punkish gear. As a joke, I asked if he was entering, because he mirrored a scarecrow. Moreover, he spoke a little like Worzel Gummidge. With a look of disgust, he pointed out he was into anarchy, whatever that meant.

People often harp on about the good ole days when there was a community spirit and you could leave your front door open and to all and sundry. If that were true, it applied long before I was a dot on the landscape. However, the celebrations were special. Folk met for the first time, and young and old literally partied in the street. Rarely have I experienced that feeling in the United Kingdom since, however London 2012 came close.

Jim appeared grown up, but could have been 13. Hanging out with his younger brother that summer, we raided his vinyl collection. One that intrigued had a blue cover with 'God save the Queen' obscuring a woman's face. Dan plonked it on the turntable. Blown away after the initial chord, at last, I had unearthed a glorious blast of rebellion. The song was top of the charts, despite the BBC refusal to air the track they deemed offensive. For they had a point, you cannot call Her Majesty a moron!

Punk had a lasting effect on my psyche, but I realised I would never snarl and lived in anticipation of a more glamorous fashion to follow. The term 'popular culture' is self-explanatory. Positivity sweet, negativity fades like love without oxygen. In hope, I awaited the messiah, the man I wanted to become, but unbeknown to me he had been and gone!

August 16th 1977 was the school holidays, and I had overslept. I trudged into the kitchen, wondering what sugar filled treat to eat for breakfast. Mum and Dad stood looking sullen and mentioned Elvis had died. The information was a flicker on my radar. The name a mystery, I assumed they meant Evel Knievel, the motorcycle stuntman. Maybe he had an accident performing superhuman feats on his motorbike. My yearning for the past was born on that sad day, two decades after the cultural whirlwind swivelled into teenagers' hearts.

As soon as I saw the broadcast on the television, I recognised the handsome youthful singer before the picture shifted to a bloated, tired older guy. The contrast was hard to comprehend. Steve Austin, the Bionic Man, was a blond version of him in younger times, a superhero that could run at 60 miles an hour in slow motion. In the playground, we mimicked him while humming the theme tune.

In the UK, we had three television channels, BBC 1, BBC 2 and ITV. Often there was nothing to watch during daytime. For hours, I longed for a programme to appear. I wondered who the girl was in the test card and if she lived inside the TV. Once as I sat waiting for it to change, a woman in a sympathetic tone announced they were to show a film in honour of Elvis the king. An American monarch no wonders he had so much jewellery!

The following morning, after playing football with mates, I tuned in once again and there he was in another movie. A singer and an actor, his lifestyle must have worn him out, and in retrospect, those thoughts were close to the truth. As I watched the flick, Dad walked in with a smile. Yet his manner surprised me, as he did not approve of me watching the goggle box during the daytime, preferring me to be outside or studying. Mum said I would get square eyes and I believed her. On this occasion, instead, he enjoyed the experience with me, while he spoke of the artistic impact the American made.

The next day after go karting along the pavement in our wooden chariots, my mates and I dashed home early to catch yet another Presley classic. Remember, we had no video recorders in those days, and if we missed something it could be years before a rerun. Huffing and puffing, having carried my mean machine up the hill, I pulled my shoes off in the hall in break neck speed. Whilst humming the Six Million Dollar Man melody, I dived into the lounge hoping the TV wouldn't take five minutes to warm up before curtain call!

Ready to tune in, I spotted Dad working outside looking at his wristwatch. I waited to see if he was to join me. Two minutes before King Creole appeared he strode in more than eager to let me enjoy the movie. The screen flickered and the words 'Paramount Pictures' emerged in black and white. Creoles sang on an empty street and trumpets rang out to welcome us to New Orleans before the legend burst into song. Hooked for life his acting performance was mesmerising!

A month later, Marc Bolan died and his songs dominated the airwaves. Back then, I mixed him up with David Bowie who warbled of space, Mars and stars. The 20th Century Boy and the Starman set the soundtrack to my childhood, and resonated as if from another planet. The everyman sells if cool. Hollywood aided Presley's appeal. Cinema was and still is a powerful publicity machine. He played a singing barman, a soldier, a helicopter pilot, a doctor, a driver, a boxer, and even a writer, to cite a few. If I could dream, I could redeem my soul and fly!

The movies were on every day during August, sometimes two clashed on both channels. Heck, he starred in over 30. The pre colour flicks, I considered his best, for they went downhill after Blue Hawaii. The cartoon 'Top Cat' I liked as a child. The Tomcat spoke like Tony Curtis, a huge matinee star in the fifties, and a story in my local town during that time made the national press. A school suspended a student for having the same hairstyle. The Jailhouse rocker dyed his locks black as homage. Second to that, he thought it would work on screen. Life is a series of repeats and copycats. Nobody is original, although Mr Sideburns was close.

A store in Ipswich had an Elvis Presley carpet on display for years. Peculiar quirks in a town I live. A common vocabulary and the Atlantic Ocean divide us from Americans who refer to trousers as pants. Here, we call them underwear. The word bum likewise has a strange connotation, and I always laughed thinking they had a comical grasp of English. When the Hillbilly Bopper sang of shaking a chicken in the middle of the room, it confused me somewhat. Nevertheless, it sounded great.

The flamboyant singer could have found us rural folk charming. Colonel Tom blocked his visit to our shores. Nevertheless, I have heard a rumour that he called on Tommy Steele in 1958, after flying in via RAF Mildenhall in my home county, Suffolk. Closed for renovation, it was a perfect spot. No press or unwanted attention, he could have flown in under the radar. There would have been no point in him visiting Wales in the seventies, cos within a few years they had Shakin Stevens rocking the valleys in his cardigan.

A few weeks after the Flaming Star died, I was at the park with friends. Stan an older mate emerged from a different neighbourhood. Three separate districts surrounded Maxie Fields. A journey of a mile by car was a few hundred yards on foot across the grassland. The news hit Stan hard, and he was saving up to visit Memphis. We had not seen him for a while, and he had greased his hair back with cycle oil and resembled the Fonz. When I got home, I poured a can over my head hoping to become a greaser.

Mum took ages to wash the gunk out with Vosene shampoo and struggled to comb knots out of my curly bonce. A parted fringe I hated and messed it up at every opportunity. Haircuts I dreaded. Dad used to take me to the barbershop full of old men. The bloke always pulled my ears to create a style opposite to what I wished. This was the decade to avoid adults with scissors, and worse still pudding basins.

We admired Stan and had no hassle from bullies in his company. Although he was tough, he never needed to prove himself. Nothing fazed him and he knew of weird and wonderful facts we had never comprehended. Once I discovered a hedgehog curled up and tried to get it to walk. He berated me and said it was hibernating as he picked it up and placed the creature in a safe spot. If we accidently kicked our football in someone's garden, he leapt the fence however high to retrieve it, in one stride.

Clever as he was, we sometimes tricked him. Once he declared with glee that he planned to watch, 'The King and I' that evening. Therefore, instead of telling him of his mistake, we kept quiet. Yul Brynner starred and Gran loved the musical. Next time we saw him we asked of the film. He complained the hero was a bald bloke and Presley never showed. I laughed so hard my ribs hurt. He was self-deprecating. A lesson I learnt and used in later life.

In the here and now, I cannot imagine a world without the Internet, mobile phones and rolling news coverage. Our neighbours had been away on holiday when Elvis died. Their son was a year younger than I was and we often chatted over the garden fence. Incredibly, 48 hours after the story broke they had no notion of his demise. Within minutes, the hits blasted from their kitchen and continued for days, much to my dad's disgust as he was on night shift.

The motion picture 'Grease' became a mammoth hit and fifties nostalgia big. Olivia Newton John, who starred in the movie, looked stunning, and I was shocked she was thirty years old. Paramount filmed one scene the day Elvis passed away. Stockard Channing sang with a poster of him in the background. The producers had considered asking him to play the part of a teen angel before his death. For obvious reasons it would have been a heart-breaking epitaph and thankfully, they signed Frankie Avalon instead.

Local kids inspired by the greasers painted the phrase 'T Birds' on the back of their jackets with liquid paper. The inventor of the correction fluid was the mother of Michael Nesmith from the band The Monkees. I wonder if she ever contemplated using it to alter the group's misspelling. Tenuous links are intriguing. Hank Marvin, guitarist with the group The Shadows commented on how many punk rockers appeared at their concerts. He asked a youth why. The lad said rock-and-roll was three chords in its purest form.

Dad bought his first Hi-Fi around this time. Before then he had a turntable, and this monster was a symphonic leap in technology. Two large speakers hung on the living room wall and it included a tape player and a graphic equaliser. One day, the sound of an opera singer's voice bellowed from the walls as he dived to press the record button. Hell, I had no idea what the woman was singing, but she was sweet on Wagner and would die for Beethoven. Within seconds the penny dropped and The Electric Light Orchestra shook the house to Rockaria! Tupelo's finest would have approved.

Political unrest never crossed my mind growing up in rural Suffolk. Locked in a bubble of a few square miles, I bought chips wrapped in yesterday's news. Ten days before my birth, a gunman murdered Martin Luther King in Memphis, Tennessee, a place synonymous with Presley. The spokesman for civil rights declared in front of thousands of people, he dreamed of a better world. Songwriter Walter Earl Brown wrote 'If I can dream' as a tribute. Presley sang it on his 1968 TV comeback show. Full of emotion he stated he could no longer sing a song, or make a movie, he did not believe in ever again.

He loathed his later films, but I enjoyed them as a youngster. They may have damaged his career, but I am sure they ensured his legacy. Today he is just as influential as he was 50 years ago. In a hurry to grow up and chase girls, I found it was to be more difficult than the lad from Tupelo had suggested. Stan and I whilst on the recreation ground impersonated the star. In our Suffolk twang, we sang 'Blue Suede Shoes' whilst wiggling our legs inside baggy trousers. Jim, our older punk friend was not there. He suffered an illness called adolescence and was feeling pretty vacant!

An echo of a world I knew so long ago, Elvis shaped my path on the marathon ahead for a moment. For thirty years, my hairstyle has been a nod to the legend, albeit shorter today. It is a life time study to find out who you are. Yet the real people who have influenced my journey have never left the building. They have walked beside me through the streets of Ipswich. Friends, family, heroes and villains of whom some are dead and some remain. One was my friend Stan, whom I knew as a boy and a man.

Castle Hill

'The only thing that interferes with my learning is my education.'

Albert Einstein

Whilst writing this book, recalling childhood events from 40 years ago has been an arduous pursuit. When I was a boy, I dreamt of a ticket to the Moon. Seldom do I venture through the estate I once lived. Thus, I figured a run to check out old haunts would help. The following Sunday was a beautiful new day, as the sun shone without a cloud in sight. Garmin set, and iPod on, The Electric Light Orchestra propelled forward on a journey of discovery.

Running down the avenue in familiar territory, once I hit Dale Hall Lane at mile 5, the brain clicked into overdrive. Along the winding roads where everybody once stopped to say hello beneath the blue suburban sky, the district had changed little apart from the railway bridge. Our house appeared much the same.

Those places had their moments. One of which was Broomhill, an open air pool once a hub of excitement, sadly now derelict. I recalled a lad known as Bomber, who used to leap from the highest board and span before hitting the water like a rocket. Sweating on the streets I was born to run, I looked back with no anger. Roaming with a gazeless stare, I no longer saw a baggy trouser on Thunder Road.

The Dales pub was now a charity shop, and the Thomas Eldred alehouse had disappeared. For all that, the 'Man on the Moon' drinkery survived, opened in 1969 to coincide with the lunar landing far above the world where planet earth is blue. Often I wondered who was Major Tom, who served us Coca Cola and Smiths Crisps on summer days. The taste was so sweet.

Maxie Fields was the recreation ground in Castle Hill, we named after the gangster in the film 'King Creole'. The suburb in Ipswich has a unique biography. A Roman Villa once stood somewhere in the vicinity long ago. My classmate Frank became obsessed with this information after getting a metal detector. For a while, we lost our pal, who dug up grass with a trowel whilst we played footy. In retrospect, he would have had to dig a great deal deeper. Today he drives a JCB!

The past as a kid was a box of jigsaw pieces strewn across the living room floor with bits missing. So many things we misunderstood. Yet the fables and yarns we heard often had a grain of truth. In 1948, the curator of the Ipswich Museum excavated the site before building the Crofts estate in the fifties. The artefacts Basil Brown found are on display in the town's gallery.

In the 2000s, the Time Team TV show visited the district with host Tony Robinson. They located the villa that now rest under houses in Tranmere Grove and Chesterfield Drive. The residents were incredibly obliging to let the archaeologists quarry their gardens. If I travelled to the past and found Frank, I would tell the little dude to search closer to home.

Our house in the heart of our street was 600 metres from where the TV show was investigating. That is not that far as the crow flies, one lap and a half of an athletics track. I used to play and dig at the top of our garden, often finding splinters of pots I discarded. Who knew what lay beneath our feet? The lawn on a slope dropped with a step in the middle. A strange anomaly and the patio flooded as water rose from the ground. A few fragments of the puzzle fit together now.

Stan was a character full of zest and curiosity, a street fighting man who talked of nature and history. Once I suggested a break from football and a trip to the shops to buy sweets. He had other ideas. Before long, we were picking blackberries. The most important tip was to pick the higher ones uncontaminated with dog pee. The lad was a real-life David Bellamy, or Bear Grylls to younger readers. One thing I learnt was never to eat conkers unless wanting to be sick. He got that wrong, mind you I did not see him consume any!

A river of metaphorical memories flowed throughout my nostalgic jaunt, as I listened to the tracks of my years. Way down at the bottom of Larchcroft Road, a red post box sparked a memory. In 1977, utter madness broke out after the school holidays, whilst The King was top of the charts. There was a conflict between two high schools over territory, and this was the contested border between districts. A plaque should mark the spot, with an inscription 'They shall not pass'.

Back then, every 10-year-old took an intelligence test known as the Eleven-Plus. Those who passed moved on to grammar school and the rest secondary modern. When I was nine, the big wigs ditched the exam that was one ugly brick in the wall. An older mate failed and to rub salt into the wound, his twin brother succeeded. Despite this, he did well, but employers were reluctant, as he had not attended the superior institution. The past is a foreign land, where Spitfire thought me stupid for writing with a left hand.

Chinese whispers swept around the playground. There was to be a fight between the schools, and the news spread fast. Frank, concerned at the prospect of being duffed up after lessons, told Mrs Peters. Yet I cannot quote the real conversation because the dude got a rollicking for industrial language. Funny as hell, the plea fell on deaf ears. There was a 15-minute eye of a storm before the big kids hit the outdoors. When the bell rang, even the toughest lad scarpered. Stan, a year older, headed out to engage in the conflict, but I doubt he knew which side to take.

When home, I told Mum of the predicted riot. Minutes later, 300 youths rampaged past the window from Thurleston High. As I tried to get a view of the action, she pulled me away from the windowsill, not wishing to attract unwanted attention. A few had school ties round their heads and gathered at the supposed district border, symbolised by the mailbox. Imagine Tucker Jenkins and the cast of Grange Hill. The grammar lads from Westbourne marched through Ashcroft Road, where many police houses stood. It was a tactical error and a few off-duty coppers depleted their numbers somewhat.

Urban myths spread around Dale Hall Primary the next morning. Some said 400 stormed the streets, and others reckoned on a teen rampage of 500. Frank insisted that a neighbour called the army, and we took it as gospel. There may have only been 30 lads that day, childhood memories are not always reliable. Another skirmish started on the allotments. Kids used onions as hand grenades, and elderly fellows outnumbered but not out gunned defended crops with pitchforks, in a rear-guard action mirroring Rorke's Drift.

Naïve compared to youngsters today, we accepted a Jackanory of a tall tale without question. If I wished to find a fact, I asked an adult, a friend or sought the library, and pal's knowledge of the alien species 'girls' was dubious. Grandad had a splendid series of encyclopaedias published in 1953, but when I looked up Elvis, glam rock, and Neil Armstrong, I was in for a disappointment.

The one medium that was uncensored was pop music. Johnny Rotten screamed there was no future and Paul Weller sang of a modern world, where the teachers said he would be nothing. The land of the young man sounded depressing. Hell, The King danced, smiled and had a party. No wonder Jimmy the punk was so miserable. Howbeit, week's later good news lifted his spirits, and grammar school beckoned. How did he cope with the dress code? Easy, our friend became electric, flattened his hair, wore a narrow tie, and followed Gary Numan.

When Star Wars the motion picture came out and caused a sensation, a pal brought several fluorescent ceiling lights to the rec to adopt as light sabres. His old man went nuts, as he had a kitchen to fit the following weekend. From that day forth, we knew him as Darth Vader, and we stayed away from his garage for eons.

Go karting vast slopes like grease lighting, burning up the quarter mile, was a thrill. The hill was a modest incline 40 years later. A few of us had karts that our dads had built. Mine was superb, a wooden plank on pivots, with a length of rope to steer. The mean machine sits in my parents' garage, with the figure nine painted on the front to this day. Blinks, a younger pal, had a L-plate on his kart. When I inquired why, he declared it stood for British Leyland. We named him that because he blinked when nervous, and I believed the explanation for the learner sign.

Airfix models I enjoyed, piecing together plastic parts and creating a mess with miniature pots of paint. Proud, I took one to school without knowing what plane it was. On the journey homewards, I wielded it above my head, making whooshing sounds. A man stopped me in the street. Imagine Michael Caine in the flick 'Get Carter', he had that look. Mr Micklewhite informed me it was a Flying Fortress, an American bomber seen soaring over Ipswich during World War 2.

Blinks and I carried replica toy pistols with gun caps that made a racket startling older folk. Once we jumped out from behind a shop, mimicking Starsky and Hutch. A woman dropped her shopping as we fired off rounds of ammunition and then chased us with an umbrella. A red car with white panels drove around our neighbourhood. I doubt it was Starsky's Gran Torino, but a customised Ford Popular.

We cycled with playing cards clipped to our back wheels with a bulldog clip. The noise against the spokes created the sound of a motorbike, and I was Evel Knievel. Often we chased Stan firing at him with toy guns. If captured, he surrendered with his arm aloft mirroring Steve McQueen whilst we hummed the theme tune to 'The Great Escape'. He feared nothing, including the battle of the schools. The kid had a slight grey strip in his hair, which I considered unusual. He smoked, drank far too much Cola, and mumbled in metaphors. If we begged him for a cigarette, he refused not wanting to lead anyone astray.

However, once he got Frank and me into real bother whilst cycling to the chippy. For some unknown reason he yelled insults at a passing jogger before shooting off, having planned a getaway. Not foreseeing the outburst, we reacted slower when the

Dave Bedford look-a-like turned and gave chase. Standing up on my racer, I could sense the chap was close. Just as I felt his palm on my shoulder, he slipped. Twenty years later, history would repeat itself when the runner chased me around a local half marathon. Later I learnt that Stan was his younger brother. Top bloke, and today I can see the family resemblance.

Our older pal smoked and did not play footy much, but if bored he dropped his cigarette and dribbled round everybody and scored. Everything appeared natural to him. While sharks circled, he retreated to the touchline, lit up a smoke, and surveyed the landscape as if a security guard. He reckoned scouts from Manchester United wanted him, but did not fancy the move because it was grim up north.

Stan did not carry a toy gun and told me the Waffen-SS captured his father in 1943. When I asked of his dad's trauma, he declared he never uttered a word on the subject. I surmise he forbade him from having a replica pistol. In hindsight that is likely and understandable.

Mum sewed my favourite number on my football jersey. Some used marker pens to their parent's annoyance. Most of my classmates went to each other's birthday parties as youngsters. Frank's dad started taking a gang of us to the park for a match, before we headed back to his house for 'pass the parcel' and jelly and ice cream. Such a popular event, other parents copied. He saw little of his father because he worked away on the oil rigs. Howbeit, when he was on leave, he often turned up for a kickabout.

Although we were young, we could tell the old fella was a superb footballer, as he juggled the ball on his head. At first, he disliked Stan because he called him Ralph Coates, a Spurs player noted for his balding hair and comb over style. Post Argentina '78, he renamed him Archie, after the Scot who scored a worldie against Holland. Frank Senior no longer had an issue with him after that and loved the backhanded compliment.

There was excitement at my hometown club Ipswich a few weeks thereafter when they faced Arsenal. Columbia Pictures filmed football sequences for the film 'Yesterday's Hero' in the interval. To make it convincing, they encouraged supporters to applaud. Sudbury, a local (non-league) team, played the fictional opposition. Filmmakers wanted actor Ian McShane to score goals, as he was the star. Most of the crowd noticed he looked too plump to be a professional and chanted, 'fatso!' It was obvious the scenes were at half time because when I watched the movie, I spotted myself reading a programme and munching a bag of Wotsits.

Later in life, I discovered Stan was older than I thought, born the day England won the World Cup. When we were 10, he was 12. This explains an awful lot in retrospect. Grease, the motion picture was in the cinema and his greased back quiff became more pronounced. His grey streak made him resemble the skunk in the cartoon called Pepe Le Pew. Once I alluded to the comparison, and he chuckled, but urged me not to repeat it in front of his girlfriend.

More often than not, he appeared with her sporting a dopey look on his face. Frustrated with my boyish square image, I grumbled to Mum about going to the barbers with Dad. More informed of fashion she took me instead, and the barber chopped less off my bonce. Self-conscious in the company of girls, a few years passed before my body caught up and longer before they showed any interest.

Aware the girl with the mousy hair might be at the rec, I spent more time getting ready before I left the house. Whenever she was around, my face turned crimson. Unable to focus on football, I once gazed at her and a ball whacked me on the side of the head. When she dumped him, it was a relief, as at least I could act normal again. When he was not looking, she winked to embarrass me. It was a God awful sad affair and I felt such a nerd.

My run refreshed the memory, as I cut through the playground I once played footy. Although it was a Sunday, the place was empty. If we were lads today, we might play video games and chat on social media. We were Ipswich Town supporters except Stan. We tried to persuade him to join the Tractor Boys, but it was a tough sell, because United had just won the FA Cup. My Dad took me to my first game. Hooked I was when I experienced the camaraderie. Our local team was on the rise, and it was a significant part of my childhood.

At the end of the decade, my family moved house and several pals I never saw again. I found it difficult to make new friends. My old school was five miles away, and I may as well have lived in Glasgow. We had no mobile phones or social media. One day, I was acting the goat on Castle Hill and then boom a different life. Instead of going out, I did keepie uppie in the garden, a skill of keeping the ball off the ground with the feet, chest and head. I had seen George Best do this on television, and his surname suited him.

Lost in thought what would I have said to my younger self on those streets. Kids, sprint from A to B and are forever in perpetual motion. He may wonder why I run and where I am going. Only when looking behind you discover life is not a destination but a journey. I would not have understood the wisdom that has taken 50 years to comprehend. Everything was smaller four decades later, except the old oak tree on Maxie Fields. We had both grown and I no longer needed to stand on a milk crate to see the stars.

Best of Times

Mile 6

'Stood high above the crowd I saw stars.'

Mark Lankester

George Best I discovered early in life when I found a jigsaw of the Irishman. Whilst I assembled it, a man emerged with black hair, a beard and a red jersey. Behind him was a huge billboard advertising Marlboro cigarettes. When I inquired who he was, Dad chuckled and explained he was a footballer on the run. Confused, I wondered why and where he had gone.

Near home was Whitehouse Park, and I hunted for him there. Once I asked a bloke if he was the Manchester United legend and he smiled adding, he wished he were. To escape the press, he fled to Spain when I was four. I have a brief vision of a news report showing him doing keepie uppie on a beach. I recognised the face and puzzle solved the pieces fitted.

Mum bought me a football sticker album, and I took it everywhere, collecting every season throughout the seventies. When I moved years later, my parents threw them out in a spate of cultural vandalism, albeit unintentional. The World Cup book survived slipped in a suitcase, my oldest possession, from which I learned the names of stars. A Polish player bore a resemblance to TV presenter Nicholas Parsons, Kenny Dalglish appeared boyish, and Dennis Law age 33 rather old.

Whilst Dad played local football, I looked out for the bearded footballer and even searched the club hut. He turned into my Lord Lucan. Surely, at 26 he must kick around somewhere. The wooded cabin smelt of mud and stale smoke. Blokes puffed on cigarettes and studded boots echoed. Watching my father yell and wave his arms for 90 minutes, I guessed he was a decent player. The ref blew on his whistle often and appeared to be an important person. The pastime looked a stressful business. No wonder Bestie had scarpered!

Footy shirts were a classic design without sponsors' names on them. Number one the goalkeeper and nine the centre forward. Dad said the old footballs were heavy when wet and painful to header, more so if you caught the lace that tied the outer skin. Never mastering the art, I closed my eyes as the leather ball ricocheted off my bonce.

The sport in the seventies was tough and unforgiving. Best never wore shin guards, and the treatment he suffered from defenders was appalling. A bloke dubbed Chopper cut him in half in one match, yet keeping upright he pulled off a worldie. Thank goodness, those wonderful moments survive on film for perpetuity.

In recent times, a modern day referee David Elleray watched a video of a seventies game between Chelsea and Leeds United. By today's standards, he suggested sending off six players. Dad stopped playing at 32 with back trouble. He did well on those bumpy pitches and I was glad he never faced The Anfield Iron, Bite your legs Hunter or Chopper Harris. Maybe George had backache wherever he was and feared doctors!

On February 1st, 1975, I went to my first professional game in expectation of another park match with a few onlookers. In the stadium, the atmosphere was extraordinary. Thousands of people went crazy, Ipswich won, and the games thereafter morphed into a collage of memories.

That season Town came close to winning the league. After three gruelling FA Cup quarterfinal replays against the mighty Leeds, manager Bobby Robson rallied the troops to face West Ham in the last four. However, the ref disallowed two perfectly legitimate goals and I never visited the Twin Towers, discovering life was not always fair.

Back then, children stood on crates and wooden boxes in the stadium. I towered over adults and hung onto their every word, as locals spoke wistfully of a young lad called Kevin Beattie. The stories resembled tales of an ancient gladiator. The football was likely the first occasion I heard an adult swear, and folk often berated ref Clive Thomas, embittered over the missed trip to Wembley!

Working-class men and boys dominated the crowd, and many brandished big wooden rattles, otherwise known as ratchets. During the Great War, soldiers used the implements to warn of gas attacks. ARP warders adopted them again in the second campaign. Strange how things evolve, perhaps a lad found one in a cupboard and took the rattler to the footy. Authorities no longer allow large items in stadiums, flares included. Good move because when I was a kid, I dreaded wearing the ill-fitting trousers.

Sport a metaphor for life, analogies such as mullered, I often use when tired after a run. Gerd Muller was a German striker and one of the finest footballers of a generation. Nicknamed 'The Bomber' he scored the winner to knock England out of the world's greatest tournament. I suspect it is where the expression originated. Great players survive on video for the future generation to appreciate. Kevin Beattie was in this class, and if you do not remember, ask an older fan or check out a DVD.

Bobby Robson said Beat was the best player he managed, a compliment considering the talent he oversaw. With the obligatory long hair of the era, he surged forward from defence faster than a steam train. In 1975, against West Ham at home, Kev ran from his own half and scored leaving Hammers trailing like skittles. For England against Scotland that same year, he bagged another goal with a fantastic header, from a Keegan cross. On the cusp of greatness, the future was bright.

The joy in the ground was electric when Kev got himself fit for action. During one game, Frank sat near us with his father home on leave from the oil-rigs. His old man fancied himself as a pro. Getting on in years, I presume the last time he played Tom Finney was at his peak. The whole afternoon, he had taken it upon himself to berate the referee, the manager, and the opposition.

In the meantime, Beattie made a brilliant tackle and belted the ball in our direction. Frank's dad leapt up to head it back, and it knocked him out cold. Ralph Coates hairstyle a mess, he collapsed over his seat. The St John's Ambulance arrived to take him away, and he never returned. Dear me, Stan gave him tremendous stick on Maxie Fields thereafter.

On September 14th, 1977, I was very lucky to be club mascot when Robson's team played Landskrona BoIS in a UEFA Cup. My name appeared in the programme stating Beattie was my favourite player, and at last, I was to meet my hero. On the day, I travelled to the ground with family, arriving at the main reception naively assuming I would change with the players. I thought we had the finest team in the world, and within a few seasons, it was reality.

Dad was as star struck as I was. In the boot room, the smell of muddy boots and liniment wafted through the air. The same aroma from when he played. He was on first-name terms with the club trainer. He did not know him and maybe he was nervous. Cyril Lee gave me a replica kit to wear, and a pair of socks borrowed from Alan Hunter, so large I could have worn them as leg warmers.

Big Al was an outstanding player, and old school hard man, making 57 appearances for Northern Ireland. Once I saw him score an own goal from the halfway line. Putting his arms aloft, he turned and smiled, as if to say sorry. Supporters soon forgave him. The Beat scored a similar one in the right end against Leeds. Bobby nicknamed them 'bacon and eggs' a perfect defensive partnership.

Before kick-off, I stood with club captain Mick Mills. In excitement I scampered straight out onto the pitch and arrived in the centre circle, surrounded by 30,000 souls, not realising teams walked out in European games. They only ran out in league matches and the players joined soon afterwards. The noise breath taking, the blood pumped through the veins. Years later, I realised the sensation was adrenaline.

Ready to play, for a minute, I felt lost. Paul Mariner, England's striker, came to my rescue before a significant UEFA match and spent his entire warm up looking after me. He took me to the goal, where I fired shots at 'Super Cooper' the keeper. Few footballers scored penalties against him back then. Saving them was his specialty, but he let me score.

Just before the whistle, I hung out with the two team captains and officials as they exchanged club pendants. The photo now sits in a draw at home. The referee tossed a coin and Mick Mills shouted heads. I asked the ref for it, as I heard you could, yet I do not think the Russian understood. The sweets shop on Dales Road did not accept rubles anyway.

Behind the dugout, my parents and sister waited with supporters and minutes before the battle started, I joined them in the expanse of smiling faces. Trevor Whymark from Burston in Norfolk scored four goals to help Ipswich win 5-0, and it was a memory of a lifetime. A bearded Kevin Beattie played that day, and I did not recognise his disguise, it were only 40 year thereafter I realised, when catching a YouTube video of the game, spotting myself in a brief foray of fame.

Kevin earned nine England caps, but should have had a ton, whilst knee problems blighted his career, battling injury. He was a tough tackler. So valuable was he to the team, they often pumped him full of painkillers before matches. Sports science was in its infancy, unaware of the long-term effects. An older supporter remembers an incident in which Kev dislocated his shoulder. A trainer ran on and slipped it into place, as he lent against the post, one of plenty of similar incidents.

The sense of anticipation before a game was spine tingling .If Kevin was fit to play, the crowd roared with delight chanting 'Beattie is back'. In the former Churchman's stand behind the goal, you could smell thick cigarette smoke and beer. Opposite was the North Stand where a thin cordon of police divided the home and away fans. From where I was, it looked like a black line moving amongst the sea of humanity.

Sometimes I spent more time looking at the vocal engine of support than the match. The word 'attack' rang out around Portman Road. The sound must have been intimidating as the mantra tailed off with an arrrrgh, as Suffolk folk mocked their visitors.

Stood behind metal railings, I clung to the barriers for dear life in case my milk crate flew from underfoot when Ipswich scored. Supporters at the back of the stand banged on the corrugated iron with fists, and once, I turned to see an old bloke of 40 wielding a boxing glove tied to a stick, smiling a toothless grin. I surmise he lost his teeth fighting opposition fans over the years, and subsequently retired to become a drumbeater. It sounded great, and in the era of bubble perms and glam rock, it was primal and thrilling.

Standing on the terraces was a profoundly different experience to that of today. Perhaps the most salient contrast was the condition of the uneven and muddy pitches. Sometimes you could not see the white markings during the winter. Players finished games covered in mud, and the skilful ones stood out. If a player strung a few passes together, folk broke into applause. The back-pass rule slowed play, and long-balls because of the conditions, were more prevalent.

Ipswich reached the FA Cup Final in 1978 and played Arsenal, whom critics considered the stronger side, despite Town finishing third in the league the preceding season. The Gunners were eighth. Thousands converged on the capital that day. My family and I watched along on the television. Beattie and Hunter having passed fitness tests, was a huge relief for supporters. Local boy Roger Osborne, on the fringe of the first team, was in the starting 11. An energetic lad, he had marked the legendary Johan Cruyff off the park when Barcelona visited.

Arsenal had a striker called Malcolm McDonald, renowned for his sprinting ability. He had competed in the TV show 'Superstars'. Every Ipswich Town supporter knew our Kev was quicker. Beattie once challenged him in a charity race, but lost, sighting issues with his shorts. He was forever unlucky. We hoped for the kind hand of fate at Wembley.

When the final kicked off, Hunter kept Super Mac quiet. The match was frantic, and both sides had chances. Early on, the Beat slid in for a challenge, and straight away, we saw him hold his dodgy knee. We prayed. Paul Mariner hit the crossbar with a shot, and a sigh permeated the air in Castle Hill.

Grandad complained that Willie Young was a dirty player, and Dad fed up with the ITV coverage, turned over to the BBC. Clive Woods our flying winger caused havoc amongst the opposition defenders. Osborne and Talbot, Suffolk lads born and breed, were busy running their socks off in midfield, and the boys looked the better team. Pat Jennings, the Arsenal keeper rushed out to stop Woodsy at one point, and slid on his back along the touchline, covering his shirt in white paint.

The management had devised a strategy to put the opposition under pressure. The Super Blues hit the post a couple more times, and we feared a sucker punch. Kevin Keegan, England's finest, said he wanted Ipswich to win when speaking at half time. I am sure every neutral supporter agreed.

Then it happened! I get emotional whenever I see a replay. In the 77th minute, David Geddis beat Sammy Nelson with his pace. The plan had worked. The teenager crossed the ball, and local lad Roger Osborne scored to make it 1-0, and then collapsed on the hallowed turf with exhaustion.

Bobby's boys were victorious and champions of football's finest football tournament. The Town Hall held a civic reception for our heroes. I was lucky to have my photo taken holding the trophy. The picture is in my parent's album. We chased the open-top bus, and it was chaos. I could see nothing but heard everything. People sat on roofs and hung out of windows. Suffolk was alive!

Miracles happen and dreams come true. On a November day in 1979, George Best arrived at Portman Road in a blue Ipswich shirt. He was only 33, and it was manager Bobby Robson's testimonial match. There were glimpses of his greatness, and I had found the roaming star, though sad and somewhat lost. When I became an adult, I understood all too well. Now a journeyman, I prayed the club owners, the Cobbolds, would take him for a pint and grab his signature, to secure the final piece of the jigsaw and a Suffolk   revolution.

If I can dream

········

Mile 7

'If you count your chickens before they've hatched,
they won't lay an egg.'

Bobby Robson

If a man can dream, he will free his soul and fly.

Paper comes from trees that pen the words. As I glance at the crumpled notebook beside me, I write of heroes from the town I cherish. In my mind I try to rewind, we have wandered so far. Blinks moved to Australia. If you requested a spot on a map, from where we rose, on Maxie Fields in Castle Hill stands a lonely Oak that watched us grow. When Ipswich won the FA Cup, a solitary blue and white scarf fluttered from its branches for months. The tree's limbs point in every direction, offering a symbol to a tribe of pals who took diverging paths when video killed the radio star.

Saturday, March 1st, 1980, times were a changing. Now at high school, music and football dominated. I was crestfallen the lure of Portman Road never seduced George Best, who chose the glamour of Scottish side Hibernian. The Irishman may have once missed a game after a night out with singer Debbie Harry, top of the charts with her band Blondie, if true, what better excuse for a sickie. 'Star Trek: The Motion Picture' launched into cinemas, and our footy team were boldly writing themselves into folklore.

Manchester United, second in the First Division, rolled into East Anglia, determined to quash the Suffolk revolution. My pal and I showed up early and invested in a match programme for 25 pence. Alan Brazil featured on the cover, scoring against the seagulls of Brighton. Inside, I purchased a pack of chewing gum, a quirk that has stayed throughout my life. The habit has contributed to a healthy set of teeth. Seldom do I frequent the dentist.

Stood in the Churchman's end, the ground was near full, in the hour before kick-off. Heavy cigarette smoke permeated the air, woven with an aroma of beer and burgers. We noticed many rival fans in our section. Not an everyday occurrence these folks were local, much to the majority's irritation. One-half of the North Stand, packed with Mancunians, chanted of the glory of the red army. A few locals copied, and we could not wait for Bobby Robson's boys to silence the lambs.

The unavailability of John Wark was a blow. The Scot surged forward from the ranks akin to William Wallace to strike fear in defences. Nevertheless, with Kevin Beattie defending our pride, we were optimistic. Dutch duo, Muhren and Thijssen ran the midfield with the finesse of nobles on horseback. Captain Mills held the central role and Eric Gates the dancing gnome fired cannonballs from 30 yards. The

Mariner, England's Number 9, pounced if a blast ricocheted.

The contest kicked off, and within minutes the young Alan Brazil nicknamed Pele, scored and Suffolk roared. Atmosphere electric, the hostility was palpable with so many locals supporting the side from the north-west of England. I felt smug that I supported my country cousins. Soon afterwards, The Beat struck with a bullet header that sailed over the bar as 'Beattie is back' chants spread across the terraces.

Paul Mariner, who looked after me when I was a mascot, scored two more goals to make it three within half an hour. Howbeit, Gary Bailey performed heroics, saving a trio of penalties for the visitors. His father played in goal for Ipswich during the sixties. With little to celebrate, the northerners chanted for the blonde-haired goalkeeper.

The Super Blues in cruise control, I turned around to watch the sea of humanity. Grown men had the joy of small children at Christmas etched across faces, and I saw an old boy wipe away a tear. At the back of the stand, I spotted Stan wearing a red scarf, looking forlorn. I had not seen him since I moved from Castle Hill 18 months earlier. I wanted to speak to him. Unfortunately, I could not move as I swayed with folk that exhaled a Saxon roar across the River Orwell.

At the interval, we ambled over to talk to Stanley, who was arguing with another lad. He followed us to the front of the stand after the heated debate, dumping his scarlet neck warmer on the terrace steps. The partisan local support shocked him somewhat on his first visit. He looked older with shorter hair, resembling a member of the popular pop band Madness. Soon he chanted that he couldn't read and write, but could drive a tractor. The penny had dropped. Home is where the heart is.

Alan Brazil produced goal four after the interval, and dis-united defenders chased Eric Gates as if he was an escaped chicken. Their rear guard in tatters, the supporters promised to keep the red flag flying high. Yet when Thijssen weaved through the defence to net a fifth, and the not so ancient Mariner sailed in with a hat trick, the vocal engine faded to grey.

Afterwards, as the crowd drifted off, we stayed hoping to grab an autograph. Although not a vintage Manchester United team, Town gave the Reds six of the best, a wonderful sight for a kid to behold. I hoped it inspired locals to support their home team. The grandparent rule should apply. If that were the case, Stan and I qualify. I met his dad in Maxie Fields. He spoke a Coronation Street lilt.

There was one old geezer standing nearby who resembled Rod Stewart. For most of the second half, we shouted to Rodney to give us a song. The nincompoop danced a jig after the game, swinging his scarf with a toothless smile. The greatest ever Ipswich Town team had come of age!

When I was a kid, I loved the glorious wartime escape saga starring Steve McQueen. That year the King of Cool died at 50. Imagine if there was to be a similar movie that included a football match.

Sylvester Stallone of 'Rocky' fame and Michael Caine are to star. Let us get into the realms of fantasy now. Half your local side, Pele and Bobby Moore are to join the cast. Unbelievable yes, but it happened!

When the new season began in August, David Bowie topped the charts and a few players sported shorter hairstyles. That summer half a dozen had been away in Hungary, appearing in the flick 'Escape to Victory'. The story involved allied prisoners of war taking on a Nazi team in a game of football. Several Ipswich lads had speaking parts, but editors dubbed John Wark because of his strong Glaswegian accent. The director wanted to take Russell Osman to Hollywood. I think it had more to do with his matinee idol looks than acting ability. Kevin Beattie doubled for Michael Caine in the footballing scenes, and in his spare time defeated Rambo in an arm-wrestling competition. Not alotta people know that.

Manager Bobby Robson had signed Arnold Muhren from Holland, a graceful athlete with a killer left foot. Impressed with his skill, he asked if he knew of any other Dutch maestros as good. Arnie suggested Frans Thijssen, the dribbler who became England's Footballer of the Year. The team changed to accommodate the pair and played to the lad's strengths. The duo helped turn Ipswich into the finest in Europe, with the help of a talented bunch of pros and master tacticians in our manager and coach. In addition, every outfield player was an international.

Reality hit on December 8th. John Lennon murdered on the streets of New York. The first time I grieved for someone I had never met. A misunderstood musical poet, he once said, The Beatles were bigger than Jesus. A common language divides, and most ordinary people in Britain understood those words, which had nothing to do with blasphemy. I am full of sorrow whenever I hear his ballads now.

The team from his hometown Liverpool arrived at Portman Road the Saturday after he died. Bill Shankly the scouser's manager was an inspirational soul who considered the game more important that life itself. Let me translate. The sport lifts the soul when times are hard, and today when we talk so much about people's mental health, what is wrong with that.

God, that day was emotional. Yet again, we were missing Kevin Beattie. Nevertheless, the Reds were without King Kenny, arguably the greatest in Britain. His replacement making his league debut wore the number seven shirt, a skinny lad from Wales, named Ian Rush. The biggest gate of the season, over 32,000 souls crammed into the ground to watch the beautiful game.

Beforehand Beatles hits played throughout the stadium. Supporters from home and away roared the tunes with passion. Spine tingling, it brought a lump to my throat. I only remember 'Twist and Shout'. When the crowd joined in, something extraordinary happened. Ipswich folk repeated one line and Kopites another in a duet of unity. It was organic, with a Suffolk twang and Merseybeat. Nobody lost. Only the love of football and music was victorious as I stood on those old concrete covered railway sleepers.

John Lennon sang of a Merry Christmas constantly throughout the festivities. To this day, I cannot bare the sadness and either switch it off or walk out of the room. On December 26th, aliens landed on the outskirts of Ipswich. Perhaps they heard a team from Suffolk was dominating across the universe. On a serious note, the incident at Rendelsham Forest (The British Roswell) happened 10 miles up the road. There were claims of a UFO landing.

The episode is the most famous sighting in Great Britain. The events took place near RAF Woodbridge. Sceptics dismissed the paranormal as lights from a lighthouse in Southwold. I am no authority on the unexplained. Today the woods are a tourist attraction, with a marathon held in the summer. Having never researched this, I have an open mind regarding such things. The wooded area is close to Sutton Hoo, an ancient burial site steeped in history. Nor must we disregard nearby Shingle Street, where strange happenings occurred during the Second World War.

The Blue and White Army were battling on all fronts in the New Year. Imagine Saxon King Harold Godwinson when he marched to the north of England to defeat the invading Vikings. Meanwhile, the Norman's of France arrived in the south and lay in wait on the fields of Hastings. Town just kept on winning and played 22 extra games on top of their league fixtures. The Blues set sail for European competition while our chief rivals Aston Villa rested. The team from Birmingham did not have to worry with mid-week FA Cup ties. We had beaten them three times and knocked them out of the tournament.

March 1981, Bobby's boys were on the cusp of a historic treble. In Europe, they visited six countries and played breath-taking football. For the Quarter Final, the lads travelled to France to face Saint Etienne. The team had legendary players such as Johnny Rep and Michel Platini. No one had beaten the Parisians at home for decades. Town battered the French 4-1 on the night to send shock waves through the continent, and were yet again victorious on the return leg.

A few years later, I was on holiday in France wearing an Ipswich shirt. A Frenchman told me what a monumental feat it was to beat St Etienne! The match had put my local club on the map. Sir Bobby said it was one of the greatest performances by a British team overseas. John Wark scored 36 goals from midfield in that historic campaign. He won the European Young Player of the Year and was also honoured in England.

Ipswich defeated teams from Greece, Poland, Germany, Holland, Czechoslovakia and France. When the celebrations were over, Celtic marched into East Anglia for Alan Hunter's testimonial. The Glaswegian club brought a travelling army of fans to take over the town. Although only a friendly, they wanted pit their wits against the best team in England. It was a great evening. A flood light went out in one corner of the pitch after the visitors had enjoyed hours of merriment in local taverns. Thankfully, Kevin Beattie was born just south of Hadrian's Wall, carved in the granite of Carlisle.

Sunday, the 29th of March, I was reading a Shoot magazine whilst trying to work out how Ipswich Town could win everything. The first London Marathon unfolded on the television as 7,000 runners pounded the streets of the capital. Fascinated, I took off my headphones and paid more attention. American Dick Beardsley and a Norwegian Inge Simonsen crossed the finish line, holding hands. When commentator David Coleman marvelled at the spectacle, I decided that one day I would run the noble race.

On April 11th 1981, I was at Villa Park, home of our title rivals. This time it was the venue for the FA Cup Semi-Final against Manchester City. As we drove to the Black Country in a convoy of coaches, we felt confident. I had bought a Walkman with my pocket money and Noddy Holder was screaming at me to turn the megawatts up loud, to send an earth tremor through the crowd. My heart raced with excitement.

The opposition was not the force we know today. Our players looked tired after 60 odd games. Alan Brazil was carrying an injury when he missed a sitter early on, and Tommy Hutchinson cleared a Kevin Beattie thunderbolt of a header off the line. The Beat was a constant threat, and a man possessed. Minutes from time fate dealt a fatal blow. Kev clashed in mid-air with a City player. He had broken his arm and wanted to play on regardless.

He looked in agony walking past fans on the way to the treatment room. We knew it was over, and it was to be his last competitive game for the club. With nine fit men on the field, we lost to a dubious free kick in extra time. We travelled back to East Anglia gutted. The European distraction of a dozen more games had sucked the energy out of the team.

The league and FA Cup double would have secured the clubs status in the record books along with the greats of the game. True, the UEFA Cup was a tough competition and recognised around Europe, but here on this island nation the domestic trophy was and still is the benchmark. A Liverpool supporter might agree. They have not won the top-flight English crown since 1990, whilst I write.

April 14th, I became a teenager, and once again, the Super Blues defeated Aston Villa. Four days later, I was at Portman Road to see our lads take on Arsenal. Ipswich had managed 33 successive home games without defeat. That day over 30,000 supporters packed into the ground, sure a triumph was imminent. Reality hit when we saw Beattie with his arm in a sling and Frans Thijssen was missing. When the whistle blew for kick off, we noticed John Wark struggle. Bobby Robson gambled on Eric Gates, and he too soon succumbed to injury. For once, they were vulnerable.

In the loft of my house are several dusty videos I have not seen in years. One had a highlight of that match. When the ref consulted the linesman over Arsenal's disputed goal, I saw myself in the crowd. I had my hand up above my eyes to prevent the glow of the sun from my pudgy face. It was surreal to spot myself as a 13-year-old, as I have no film before the age of 26. I looked different to what I remembered and bore a resemblance to my daughter. So much so, I could have been her baby brother.

On the last day of the season, Bosko Jankovic scored twice for Middlesbrough against a wilting Ipswich, and Aston Villa won the league. Robson's boys pulled themselves together and triumphed in the UEFA Cup, winning the two-legged tie against Dutch team AZ Alkmaar. It was fantastic, but the English premier competition was the one most fans wanted!

I do not recall the final being on television. My mate and I listened to the radio while playing Subbuteo. The commentary sounded distant, as if from another planet. The tension unbearable, we crushed several players under foot as we celebrated the win. European night games I loved. You could smell the River Orwell through a mixture of beer and cigarettes, as a mist descended over Portman Road.

While writing this book, I had a dream I was playing footy at Maxie Fields. Never superhuman when running, I am in slow motion. Alan Brazil appeared as if a ghost heading for the goal, reminding me of the opening sequence to TriStar Pictures, where a white horse with wings glides past the screen. John Wark followed, hit a skyrocket of a shot and vaulted into the air to celebrate. Ingrained into my DNA, there was never an Ipswich Town team to match them ever again.

Mr Brazil is now a professional broadcaster on the radio. A few years ago, I bumped into him in the Neptune café and reminisced on the historic period in the club's history. He relished talking and lamented on not winning the league. Big Al told me he had run a half marathon in his playing days in an old pair of Adidas Gazelle trainers. He did not enjoy the event, but I was in awe of his finish time. I wish I had asked him why he calls football supporters 'punters'. It is only a minor grievance, but I always think of gamblers. To be fair, I have rarely walked into a betting shop. Once I bet on the Grand National and the horse died before the race.

When I go to a home game today, I see ghosts of the boys of 1980/81, before the modern side runs out, and they disappear. One specific goal remains in my mind against Aston Villa. Frans Thijssen dribbled from the halfway line and started a breath-taking team effort featuring five players. Yet another splendid performance and the butterfly effect in time. Yeah, winning took its toll.

The Beat missed many games that season through injury. Howbeit, I will forever remember him coming off the bench to score a thunderbolt of a free kick, with his first touch against Bohemians of Prague. Supporters were screaming for Bobby Robson to bring him on, and I am sure they influenced his decision. The tension was electric. When he scored, people young and old gasped in disbelief, uttering words such as 'did you see that', 'unbelievable' and 'legend'. It surprised me the ball did not smash through the net, and into the terrace.

The summer of 1981 came. It was now the cricket season, and I forgot football for a few months. A star shone from the television in a grainy newsreel from the United States. A flash of brilliance as Georgie Best scored a wonder goal, weaving around countless players as if to remind us he was still the greatest.

The legendary Ipswich team was a mix of British finest with a Hook of Holland flare and Terry Butcher from Suffolk a blue through and through. There is an iconic photo of him sporting a blood-soaked head bandage representing England. However, another injury he received in a FA Cup tie at Luton in 1982 was life threatening.

Dad took me to the game at Kenilworth Road and on arrival, we popped into a café, and he bumped into an old pal. I listened with interest as they spoke of the First Division Championship winning team of two decades earlier. Afterwards, we headed to the entrance of the stadium that was a row of terraced houses. The Hatters were useful and could mix with the best. Their nickname references their trade in hat making over the years.

During the match, there was a sickening clash involving Big Tel. From where I stood, it looked awful. He tried to play on but was in distress. Later he had a blood transfusion and could have died. Ipswich Town finished second in the league again, Bobby Robson went to manage England and the dream evaporated. Butch was a legend, but his career was only just beginning.

Beattie returned to Portman Road in March for his testimonial against Moscow Dynamo. The match was a fitting tribute. I saw grown men cry, and at the final whistle, kids ran to congratulate their idol. An old Scotsman puffing on a cigarette urged me to run on the pitch. He said I would cannie see his ilk again. A statue should stand of him, but I cannot imagine this happening soon. Altered Images of childhood faded into the past and life transformed, I know that much is true. Girls become more appealing. With auburn hair and tawny eyes, the kind that hypnotise, a new order beated in my heart without surrender.

A few months after I finished writing this chapter on September 18th, 2018, Kevin Beattie died aged 64. Sad and emotional, I read back over the words I wrote and changed nothing. Yet, I have since learnt that plans for a statue are in progress and supporters are funding much of the cost. I wish we had done it in his lifetime. I met him in 2015 and told him he was my hero. That makes me happy. Rest in peace Kev, you were a diamond who will live forever in our hearts.

Changes

Mile 8

'A freckled face and hair black wet with morning dew, I walked to a different beat, a modern era dawning.'

Mark Lankester

Baby boomers dominated the population by the sixties. Wealthier than their elders had been growing up, they had the freedom to define their own identity. The boom had dwindled when I arrived in 1968. Generation X is our tag, and it has nothing to do with Billy Idol. Nor were we an afterthought, for poets rose from our crowd, revered and proud.

The youth of the sixties approached 40 by the time I was 14, and Bill the peroxide rocker was planning a white wedding. Nonetheless, a mere quarter of a century separates my parents and me, and there are memories we share from younger days where our cultural experiences merge. Howbeit by 1982, I tuned in to bands closer to my age, and it was tribal with ska, punk, and the New Romantic Movement to name a few.

Slade arrived at the Ipswich Gaumont in the spring, and off I went with Dad, despite considering the

Brummies' relicts. However, the band rocked from the first guitar chord, quicker than the records to bring the house down. Youths began head banging, and I nodded in approval and briefly dreamt of becoming a rocker, though the phase passed.

Synthesised music was the sound of the future, and Gary Numan had friends who were electric. Sunday afternoons, I tuned in to the top 40, seeking to copy songs without Tony Blackburn's rude interruption. The tape often chewed up inside the player, so to repair, I span the flimsy spools back into place with a pen. Agfa cassettes were okay and affordable, and occasionally I upgraded to TDK.

Today, when songs from the era fill the air, I expect certain tunes to follow, and occasionally I accidently pressed the red button over a pre-recorded classic. Chariots of fire extinguished Vangelis wrestling with the synthesis, and Rocky rose up to the challenge of his bible.

The day one's voice broke, I sang a Depeche Mode chorus switching from the heights of Jimmy Somerville to Phil Oakey in a second, developing a one-track mind. Altered images bringing me closer to adulthood, Claire Grogan, I wanted to date. Years later, I learnt Gary Kemp wrote a song about Gregory's girl and the words ring true.

Dad, pushing forty, kept fit by jogging. The prospect of wearing carpet slippers within a year, instead of Silver Shadow running shoes the British Army still issues to new recruits, a motivation. I tagged along sometimes for a mile or so before walking home, much to his disgust. He ran so far, and maybe the precedent set was significant.

The future had arrived, the beat never surrendered, and we walked and talked in time. Girls became women overnight, and with the music light years away from Maxie Fields, flared trousers became a distant memory. Howbeit, living in Rushmere a mirror reflected a changing face occasionally resembling a kid I once knew.

Space age sounds of Ultravox and co forged a fresh beginning, as a monster rose across the River Orwell. Concrete pillars emerged in the middle of the estuary, building a bridge to our hearts. My pal Phil and I cycled over to Wherstead Road to watch the overpass bloom. The framework took shape, as if Star Wars AT-AT armoured transporters were invading the town. The sight looked magnificent, albeit not aesthetically pleasing.

One day when the river crossing was near completion, we got chatting to a man stood staring at the structure, rubbing his chin. Although he never blinded us with science, he knew his business and asked if we noticed anything out of the ordinary. To be honest, we had no answer. Therefore, he explained the cunning plan. Engineers had built the flyover at an angle, to preserve the natural beauty of the area.

The idea impressive, the bridge appears shorter from certain vantage points. We could have been speaking to the organ girder. He resembled Tony Robinson, who played the character Baldrick in Blackadder. The

TV comedy Suffolk folks, not the pub Alan Brazil used to run. I wonder, maybe it was he himself?

The bridge opened in December 1982, preserved on celluloid later in the decade in a movie starring Michael Caine. Yet, before traffic rolled across the tarmac for freedom and pleasure, a half marathon celebrated the milestone with runners turning their backs on Mother Nature to rule the world. Sadly, I missed the parade. Thereafter, we biked over the highway in the sky during rush hour. Yes, a hair-raising experience, but we were young and foolhardy.

Sometimes we cycled miles to Felixstowe on the coast. Once, we swam out too far, and struggled to get to shore. We did not speak much of it, and when my pal threw up seawater, we brushed the episode off with the nonchalance of youth. Hell, we did not need the Hoff to rescue us, but it was a daft stunt and a valuable lesson learnt.

In 1983, aged 15, I became obsessed with the swiftly changing fashion, wearing drainpipe jeans, grandad shirts and suede shoes. Phil bought a pair of faded pin striped denim trousers. He said they made him look like he had been trendy longer. I just thought they looked old.

Wedge haircut in eyes, I cycled downhill, sparks flying off Blakey heels. Hairs dyed blonde with spray on bleach, when it grew out, in wasp like streaks, my parents were livid. Pop stars of the day set the trend and an Elvis style simpler, I felt in the wrong era.

Overnight everything changed with a New Order and a Blue Monday. The rhythm was Industrial, ultra-modern, dark and grim, as if recorded in a derelict wasteland. Imagine films of the north, showing empty steel works and shipyards. The track northern and Mancunian, on Factory Records, I had never heard of a 12-inch single the same size as an album, that ran for eight minutes.

While running I still tune into the hypnotic track, the beat pushing me for a mile, and on repeat two. The first long-play record to enter the charts worked miracles on the dance floor. Disco sounded appalling to our ears, conjuring up images of flared trousers and big collars. Repetitive rhythm helps me relax, and this I will focus on later.

Saturday mornings we ventured into town. Parrot Records our port of call, and hours flicking through vinyl, with the dilemma of choice. Break Dancing had reached the shores of Britain and StreetSounds released a series of electro albums, mixing tracks into a non-stop beat. The new craze, a blend of dance, and rap merged with a European electronic sound.

Those antiquated synthesisers, dated today, were a quantum leap from our parents' choice in music. On occasions, dressed to the nines, I visited the Fireball Disco at the Corn Exchange, and watched in awe as lads breakdanced on the stage. The girls were younger and the Swan pub across the road soon became more appealing. Sometimes, if with an older mate, we bought a pint. Hansa beer, Vikings finest, ordered with a pinch of lemonade.

One Saturday after spending hours wandering the town, Phil and I visited the local Wimpy. McDonald's was yet to dominant the high street and we ate with a knife and fork. While sat talking, we debated the fate of the Super Blues. The year before, Bobby Robson had left to manage England, Kevin Beattie had retired, and the club sold players to finance a new stand. Now a mid-table outfit, the team's future uncertain, there was no need for a crystal ball to predict the inevitable.

The Story of the Blues, they took our side, but could not take our pride. The only positive, Suffolk boy Terry Butcher staying on to captain the sinking ship. Ashes of memories still aglow when we finished eating, the heavens opened, and in no rush to get soaked with gel-coated hair we ordered another coke. An older fella in the company of a glamorous girl sat opposite, peering in our direction. He looked like Pete Wylie from the band The Mighty Wah!

Initially distracted by Blondie, the penny dropped, and I recognised the punk lad from an earlier chapter. He had changed his look, and when I nodded, he came over to talk. Soon it became clear he was desperately seeking to impress Susan at our expense, and flashing the cash, he offered to pay for our drinks.

Jim settled the cost, not realising we had eaten, and was in for a hefty bill. Meanwhile, we scuttled out into the street with 30 seconds to spare, before he discovered our unintentional deception. Soon we heard him roar and ran for our lives. We should have outrun the lad who carried a briefcase. Yet, he closed the gap, and lungs burning we hurtled uphill towards Electric House.

About to quit and take a beating, a run-away bus slowed, and we jumped aboard. To escape his malice, we held on for dear life expletives fading into the distance as we paid the conductor. I ate my ticket, and we laughed so much it hurt, adult's disapproval making the episode funnier. They were working for the rat race, wasting time, discussing the world's situation in a different frame of mind.

Conscious we were agitating the elderly we moved upstairs, and with a better view of the road saw our foe giving Alan Wells a run for his money. Fear set in and the heart raced when the driver stopped to pick up passengers. However, the last person boarded, and he gave up the chase with a two-fingered salute. I wonder what happened to his girlfriend.

The holidays may have ended in September 1983, but it was a Sunday as we cycled towards Nacton, and spotted runners on the bridge. When we arrived at Ransomes Industrial Estate, I asked a woman how far they were running. She told me the event was a marathon. I enquired if it was the same as London and she nodded in agreement.

There were a few cameras, and with a track top hood over one's head, a black-and-white photo survives. Meanwhile, I had been reading the Orwellian novel describing a future world of Big Brother and mass surveillance.

The author Eric Blair stayed in Southwold and was familiar with the river that weaves through Ipswich, the probable inspiration for his pseudonym. For today, most of us know of George Orwell. Imagine the words that could have flowed from his pen if he had seen the rise of the concrete beast. The artery of the once Saxon town may stand for millennia.

Not long after we arrived a lad pulled up on a Puch Maxi moped, and when taking his helmet off, I recognised Stan, mullet flattened by the headgear. With his trademark grey streak, he reminded me of the singer in A Flock of Seagulls, and we were envious of the machine he nicknamed putt-putt.

He was there to see his brother who finished strongly, and seconds later Jim stormed towards the finish line, legs buckling with yards to go. Fortunately, he looked in no condition to beat me up over the Wimpy incident, but it was no surprise to me he ran a marathon and we went over to congratulate the pair.

Phil left suffering from boredom, and I hovered for ages, headphones on plugged into a new romantic soundtrack morphing with the human struggle. The athletes lived through their vocation until completion as I stood there waiting. The heart never grows old. The sign led the way, and I would run the distance one day.

Events that stretched out before me were in harmony with the rhythm. Runners wore club vests I did not recognise with pain etched on every face, and the haunting tones of Vienna flowed as Migue Ure reached out in a piercing cry. Yet, when the electric masterpiece ended, Joe Dolce broke the tranquil and empty silence and told me to shaddap my face.

The Italian kept Ultravox off the top of the charts, so I knew the next track. When I shouted the deafening lyrics, I got a few looks from folk, but in the cool grey sky, they faded into the distance. Ridicule was nothing to fear, and we spent our cash on looking flash to grab a girl's attention.

Often I daydreamed as I walked past passing strangers and wondered if I would know them in the distant future. Some runners are now friends, and I remember a girl in the high street I hoped to marry one day, although we had never spoken. She was more than a beauty queen from a movie scene. This sounded nonsense, but several years later, we wed, and on the avenues we walk, every step reminds me of how we used to be.

The challenge of 26.2 miles far away, adolescence was to be a tough, challenging and emotional marathon. For now, I danced through the streets wearing the obligatory white socks of the era, avoiding the cracks in the pavement. In a flicker of one's existence, we were the kids from East Anglia running Wilde and free!

Bjorn Borg, five times Wimbledon champion, helped create a new trend with the Fila sports gear he wore on court. The brands unavailable in Britain, young Liverpool fans bought home when their team played in Europe. Soon, youths turned out in the attire throughout the country, establishing a fresh youth movement called the casuals.

By 1984, I sported white tennis shoes, Sergio Tacchini track tops, Pringle jumpers and electric blue cords. Match days was our catwalk. At Christmas, Bob Geldof reminded everybody there was more to life than music, fashion and excess. If I had jumped 30 years into future, I would have discovered myself preparing for yet another marathon, with familiar faces running through worn out places, in a mad world.

That freckled faced teenager could have taught me a thing or two. In middle age, I had become lost. If I saw him, I might inform the lad of his destiny. Slave to the rhythm, the fire burnt as he marched forwards, yet to turn his head on a path travelled. Two talking heads with the same soul I see him in the mirror daily, caught in a glow of the light.

Never lose your romance. Sip from the wine of youth once again and rise to keep it alive. Reckless and so hungered on the edge you trail, tie on your running shoes and never fail. Catch a smile from a passer-by, while blistered and broken, unable to reply. As distance heals the strongest pain, the kid I used to know, I left behind long ago in a never-ending story. Same as I ever was, a nagging doubt remains.

Manchild

....

Mile 9

'A youth pupate in chrysalism morphs as if a butterfly
shedding childhood dreams, wide-winged and in
confusion, into dark clouds and thunder; for lest we
forget we once felt the rain, the adult forgetting the
perilous trail.'

Mark Lankester

Great Scott, it is 1985 and I am a slave to the
bright and stylish rhythm of the fashion. Halfway
there, living on a pray, we danced in the streets and
wanted to rule the world. 'Back to the Future' was the
biggest grossing film of the year, as the hero Marty
McFly time travelled to 1955. He and I were both just
17, though divided by a common language.

Imagine if Universal Pictures had set the tale in
England, it would have been extraordinarily quaint
yet beautifully comic with no proms, few cars and
post-war rationing. Upon that moment long ago, so
young and carefree on the cusp of adulthood, no lad I
knew in Ipswich drove a DeLorean. Instead, we
lounged on the top deck of buses, smoking, laughing
and pontificating on life with a curious metallic musty
smell pervading the air.

The hair on my head grew quicker than weeds, and our features altered in an uncertain period concerning our position in society. For it could not last forever. The journey was living, and the destination a vivid memory. Our fathers had wandered these streets before, and for now, we dreamed uncorrupted by disenchantment.

Identity and belonging woven into human nature, the United Kingdom must mean something, surely. Miners walked with the dignity of king's and dug for black gold in the hills and valleys for generations. While we danced, they fought side by side to protect their livelihoods and communities, and the yuppie was on the rise. Football supporters were next on the hit list, according to Alex. I accepted those words with a shared cigarette and a nod without realising the foresight in those words. I was green, and everything was new, but within a year, my mood would be blue.

Alexander the Mate was our unelected leader, a tad older and educated at what we termed a posh school. He was always a stride in front on the holy grail of youth. Hell, I do not know what he studied there, because at every available opportunity he gave a rip roaring familiar speech. This happened when under the influence, and he forgot the script when sober. He was a witty chap and a product of his environment. His dad enjoyed a beer, and mum was religious. Booze was proof God wanted us to be happy, and the hangover a reminder it was temporary.

Much as we were on a journey to discover who we were as individuals, we loved music and football.

Howbeit, my deep interest in bygone times grew daily. The fascination was always there from my days listening to Grandad's stories, old movies and Stan's tall tales. I left school with O Levels in Art and History, poor subjects to have top grades in when looking for a career. Sonny Jim, you can draw and tell me of the Industrial Revolution, but are you literate in computers?

The ZX81, oh dear, I pressed a few keys and that was about the sum of my ability. I attended Sixth Form for a term and wasted my time. My first job was as an office clerk at the Ipswich Cooperative. Heaven knows I was miserable now, and I hoped to die before I got old. Deep in my heart of hearts, I pined to go to Art School as I danced through the dark, dreaming my life away until 5pm.

Clive drove a Sinclair C5, mobile phones did not exist and the nearest we had to a selfie were booths at train stations and shops. I still carry sepia snapshots the size of a large stamp in my wallet, showing a kid yet to understand adulthood in its entirety. Imagine a jogger taking a before and after snapshot. The second beams a weathered expression after the wide eyes of expectation have disappeared.

Heartache, the woman I promised myself to marry, was at the same clubs and walked the same streets. If I saw her face in a crowd, my heart skipped a beat. I had a sliding doors feeling we had met in another life. Sounds prompt memories at unpredictable moments. A song by ZZ Top flings me into a bar called Blades in Ipswich. I was under 18, as was half the pub, although if full of adolescent men, door attendants demanded identification. Fate dealt a blow every occasion I plucked up the audacity to ask her for a date. One particular night everything was going great until a bouncer asked Alex his age. Sixty-Four was the wrong answer!

Nightlife was scarce in Suffolk, but not in Essex. Laser lights shone at the Tartan House in Colchester, and this was our time. We talked until sunrise, I never felt tired. My health I took for granted, and responsibility was far away. I yearned to stay a kid forever, as adulthood dragged me forward. Six months was a lifetime and every moment I thought I had found my feet, I stumbled.

I passed my driving test in 1986. The first car I bought was a Ford Escort that I customised- hooking up the brake lights back to front. I had a sticker that advertised the Essex nightclub across the windscreen, which read, 'If it moves, funk it'. A grumpy bloke with a cig hanging from his lip informed me the phrase was 'effing offensive'.

The 12-year-old vehicle was not luxurious in the days before power steering. Most cars had manual chokes, and the plastic-covered seats got boiling hot during the summer. The police stopped me on plenty of occasions. One day Alex and I drove into a stakeout sting and two plain clothed coppers dragged us out of the car. Gordon Summers, we were in Copland, what now!

The police officer who spoke to me I recognised, he played football with Dad when I were a kid. I mentioned this, and we talked about the game for a while. Hell, all blokes are lads at heart and he shared my sorrow at Ipswich Town's demise. Alex was having a somewhat tougher integration. The fact he had asked for a 'brief' was not his best move.

I was a poor driver and sped along, taking stupid risks. The human brain's frontal lobe does not fully develop until 25. I am surprised the media do not discuss this scientific discovery more often. Inevitably, I wrote off my car, and saved a long time for another. When I returned, I was 19 and more recognisable as the man who is writing. The face now set as I shaved daily, and the quaffed hairstyle stayed for good.

Most Saturday nights we ventured into town. Phil worked in Tattingstone, on the outskirts of Ipswich. He invited our group of friends to the village disco. Now most of us had cars, we were more mobile. We looked forward to a change of routine and arrived at the hall on a balmy summer's evening.

Some of the youths resembled Status Quo. If my Suffolk dialect was a seven, these boys were a ten. Rock music played, and I recalled the Slade gig years earlier. Heavy, it was 1987, and we had stepped back in time at least a decade. Neil, a local lad, asked me if I liked Rainbow. I thought he was taking the mick, but he was referring to the band. I assumed he meant the TV show that featured Zippy, Bungle and Jeffery!

The rural guys drank real ale, and it tickled them when we ordered lager. The old boy behind the bar called it 'Nat's pee'. I enquired if the DJ's could pump up the volume with a track by MARRS. 'What planet are you on boi', the reply. By Jove, what a bunch of scruffy Herbert's we have here, where is the Champagne chaps? Alex had an Etonian humour that often backfired, but on this occasion, he had everybody eating out of the palm of his hand, especially the women.

The records they had were fantastic. Thin Lizzy, Led Zeppelin, Status Quo and The Rolling Stones rocked the hall. The music had never died. We had just ignored it, too busy following the latest trends. Yep, my pals and I had sold out and had forgotten our roots. Thank God, pound notes were still in circulation, otherwise the treasure tokens would have spilled over the dance floor. The moment Bono roared they could not take our pride, united as one our voices echoed far and wide.

Later, a few of us ventured outside the hall and talked. With the distant sound of Bob Dylan, I took in the picturesque village scene. Dressed so fine in our prime, drinking and thinking we had got it made, rolling down the hillside we discovered Lemons Hill Bridge. I wondered how life here could bore the locals as I stood there in the moonlight. Today I run around Alton Water near Tattingstone, remembering those joyous times.

In the late eighties, we were not the only ones to forget our souls. Bands over synthesised their songs and forgot the human touch. The synthesiser on 'You Win Again' by the Bee Gees echoes like a broken washing machine, as if recorded in a laundrette. Once you get that image in your brain, it is difficult to listen to it in the same light again. We thought the guitar would die and how wrong we were. Those kids in Tattingstone were not slaves to popular trends. We were the mugs!

On another occasion, we learned of a party in Newbourne, a not so nearby village. In we jumped into a friend's car and set off for an adventure, ending up at an ancient farmhouse full of Hooray Henrys. Whilst mingling, we noticed there was no music playing and Alex who should have been in his element, was strangely quiet.

My name rang out across a crowded room. Stan, I had not seen in a while. We shook hands, and I noted the silvery streak in his hair had vanished. Yep, it was a dye job. He mentioned he had been working as a plasterer. With a beer in his hand he declared, he loved getting plastered. It was surreal and the circle of life.

Dedication to the cause, he had cycled 12 miles from the other side of town. There was a strange atmosphere, definitely not our scene. Most of the youngsters appeared to be half-asleep, disorientated, and kept saying, man. The party host was Aubrey. After a few beers, we became bored and left.

Howbeit, our chauffeur had departed, and the house was phoneless. Therefore, we had to walk. Stan said he would tag along for a while. When we went outside, he peered around and yelled that a weasel had jipped his bike. This Suffolk-ism may puzzle readers. Somebody had stolen his bicycle. He was now a foot soldier.

Lost Boys creating unintentional crop circles, for hours, we walked through fields. Stanley suggested we split up in two groups of three, and he would lead one on a reconnaissance mission. I shook my head, and glanced at my mates - he had not changed. Within 10 minutes, he had tumbled into a ditch.

Somewhere in the Suffolk countryside, we voted never to venture away from our urban surroundings again. Phil moaned that the place stank and lacked shops. That was true. Eventually we located the (BT) Tower in Martlesham, a local landmark, and we knew we were close to civilisation.

There are other buildings I look for if lost, every field has its markers. When I took up running, I looked out for them. Nowadays I know the territory and no longer need guidance. When we arrived at BT, we sauntered over to a car park where two Second World War monuments stood.

Stan smiled and lit up a cigarette. He said we were on the original army parade ground, and must not forget the sacrifice people had made. He had a curious presence, as if he had lived in another era, but he was right in hindsight. All of us became more like him, as we got older. Martlesham Control Tower we discovered standing alone, surrounded by homes established in the seventies. The night evolved into a historical walk and was memorable.

Once we reached the peripheries of town, the rest broke off in other directions for a well-earned sleep. Stan had three miles further to stagger than I did. We cut across the golf course, as it became daylight. I asked if he would be okay, as he had a long trek on foot. Suddenly, I spotted his bike resting against a post box. A fellow partygoer must have pinched it, although I kept silent about my suspicions.

Without swearing about the thief, he hopped on his wheels with glee. Off he rode into the distance as the sunlight rose. 'See ya mate,' I hollered, and he spun round and saluted, just as he did when we were kids. As he predicted, buildings I remember have disappeared, some built in my lifetime. We should preserve the past; few photos or videos exist from my youth.

For the next six months, we hung out with Stan. One evening we were drinking in a local pub, long since demolished. Tonight, we risked demolition ourselves. A mate must have knocked a drink over whilst chatting to someone's girlfriends. Sozzled and easy targets, a group of irate older blokes outnumbered us somewhat. We sobered up and hoped we could talk our way out of the incident. Just as I was about to open my mouth, Stanley steamed in and the world went black for a few seconds.

Floored with the first punch, I got a fair bit of sympathy for my wounds. A girl gave me a tissue. Embarrassed, I had yet to see my blood-covered face. I did not want the aggravation of explaining my condition to all and sundry in the taxi rank. The subsequent walk home was an opportunity to clear my head. The pound coin rolled along the pavement and dropped into a drain with a plonk. Trouble followed my old pal as seagulls follow a ferry.

The next day I woke up with a hangover and made a lame excuse to Mum for my swollen lip. In those times, we always walked late at night with no fear. This was Ipswich, England, not the Wild West. From that moment on, I avoided Stan. He had never left Maxie fields. Sadly, I had almost forgotten. No longer a member of his entourage, I marched on through the plains like a metaphorical lone Ranger, the Mark I once knew now a stranger.

The winter of 1987 was a bleak period in my life as dark thoughts filled my mind. The big hair, bright clothes and over produced music only blinded me to what was going on in the actual world and the pipe dream faded as if watching wallpaper fall to show mould. Tear down the wall, feed the people, and free Nelson. The harder it rained, the less I cared. The man upstairs was crying!

On the 15th of October, a tremendous storm hit Britain. I walked back from the pub that night, unable to light my cigarette, as I pulled my coat tight to my chest. Dustbins and fences flew across the road, and when home, I slept through the cyclone that shattered windows. It was an end of an era. The next morning was a scene of utter devastation that echoed my state of mind. Britain's landscape changed forever, and so had I.

More depressive music now fitted my mood, and I quit the hype and become more insular. I did not know what was happening. I was a teenager and figured it was normal. Depression- what was that? Somcone once informed me that 18 to 21 were the best days of your life. Old age and disappointment loomed. My expectations had run dry and resentment rose high in a world where money ruled instead of the man in the sky.

Nights out with friends were a chance to drink as much as possible. I no longer cared about my health and well-being and tore myself apart as desperation took hold. An alcoholic cannot have just the one drink. That is an obsessive nature, and I assume you are born that way. Running is addictive, and it is no surprise I discovered the sport.

When at high school, I was a pudgy kid. This is not fun when you want to wear trendy clothes, so I cut my food intake. Not understanding nutrition, I had a limited grasp of the connection between physical activity and weight loss. Gradually I slimmed down, but I am sure it started there. In my late teens, I suffered frequent headaches. Often they were so bad I vomited. After being sick, it released anxiety, and the pain disappeared.

Tension appeared to trigger the attacks. They were so persistent I forced myself to throw up, to feel better. It always worked, especially after evening meals. I discovered it to be easier if I downed a pint of water beforehand. A means to cure a severe headache became an illness.

When I drank alcohol, I never forced myself to be sick as not wishing to waste the mind-numbing affect. Smoking suppressed the appetite, and my condition got worse. Soon I threw up after every meal and lost so much weight everybody noticed. Now one of the skinny lads the clothes fitted and the side effects I ignored.

Often I sat on a wall somewhere and observed the world around me. As I puffed on a cigarette, I would see middle-aged joggers desperately running to reclaim their youth. Husband and wives walked together in misery, and mothers yelled at their kids. About to give up hope I would spot a pretty girl, and perhaps things were not so bad. The smile from one and sometimes a date was as if an angel had flown into my heart to keep the fight alive.

Never fooled again, when I watch the movie 'Quadrophenia', I remember teenage angst, disappointment and the loneliness of adolescence. Jimmy the Mod drove a scooter off a cliff. The metaphor was that he became a man, not a follower, as the bike smashed on the rocks below. Life is about self-respect, not affirmation from others. If you seek kudos, you are wasting your valuable time.

When I met my wife, I was 20 and slowly sorted myself out, but never forgot those troubled times. Finally, I plucked up the courage to ask her out. Girls are far more grown up than boys are at 15, and it had taken me an eternity to grow up in five years. Besotted life changed and finally I was complete. The sun rose on her face and those clouds disappeared. I was a young old man without a dream, but now I dared to believe!

In 1989, I left home and moved into a bedsit. I had to eat, food cost money. Not having enough, I drank less, cut down on smoking and lived on toast. I would be sick once a week, then once a month, until it stopped. I never sought professional advice about Bulimia and confided in no one - this was the eighties! Girls suffered from that, and I was ashamed. I stuffed all that pain into a black box, and I was riding on high. Hang tough and be strong, because if you show a weakness now so much could go wrong.

For I found pale shelter in my tiny room, the carpets tired and shredded. A ray of light shone through a broken windowpane. The nineties loomed as I combed my hair with nothing new to wear. Nevertheless, I was not alone. Loneliness is the killer. I had met the love of my life. My tainted heart would heal with time. The boy inside became a distant memory, and when the Berlin Wall fell, I was 21 in a sweeping   wind   of   change.

Our House

Mile 10

'The adolescent who is perfectly adjusted to his
environment, I've yet to meet.'

Roger Bannister

January 1st, 1990, early dawn, white noise
disturbed my slumber as I picked out the tones of
distant cars, singing birds and the gentle pitter-patter
of raindrops. The fusion of sound hypnotic, for a
moment I did not notice the hangover and sneezed,
my nose itching against the carpet in the tiny bedsit.

For an eternity, I watched a giant spider crawl up the
wall shifting its head to stare at a passionate fool. The
one luxury I had was a colourless TV, which I turned
on and off with a snooker cue before the advent of
remote control. I seized the stick to knock the furry
creature of its stride, but out of reach, my long-legged
friend had as much right as I to walk on by.

I rose and stumbled towards the sink in the room's
corner, and splashed my face with icy water. In need
of a smoke and fresh air, I lifted the rotting window
frame, and leant into the whirling rain to numb the
pain. Unsteady on feet, hollow and weak, I spotted
my personal Jesus pecking for crumbs with a tiny

beak. The clatter of glasses from the adjacent pub and the generator from the local swimming baths creating a symphony together with English church bell chimes.

Voices in the kitchen rang out to the backdrop of sliding doors, cutlery, and hilarity, and to my surprise when I sauntered in my trio of mates were wide-awake. Logan a Scot was the oldest at 25 and the patriarch of the group, John, a classic student sort the youngest at 19 and Keith, a year older than I was, a computer whiz who ran. He encouraged me to keep fit and throughout January, we ventured out over the park. I toiled, but it was a start.

Morning folks, I yelled, and as if by magic we sang in unity, to the words of Bernard Sumner and the nineties had landed. We were a skinny crew that thrived on toast and pot noodles, but I wanted to get healthy. I appreciated the lads, but it was not a lifestyle choice. Desperate to move, I was saving for a place, and every spare bit of cash I earnt with overtime went into the building society.

Phil and I had celebrated the New Year with the girls at the Garland in Rushmere. The old alehouse was a regular hangout. Eighties music floated through the air as the young danced to the backing track of pivotal change and growth. Every Tuesday was disco night, and I took my wife there on a first date, as I snagged the odd smoke from a friend when out of view. In the 21st Century, bulldozers moved in to obliterate memories. Nothing lasts, only bygone tunes.

Living at the top of a three-story Victorian bedsit, opposite Christchurch Park was okay, and I had a comfortable armchair. The kitchen had a direct fire escape with stairs that ran to the backyard, convenient for a cig and a view of the town centre. If we spotted a passer-by, we yelled the name 'Steve' and laughed as folk spun around in bewilderment.

However, once an elderly lady dropped shopping bags in horror as apples and oranges spilled across the pavement. In a flash, I vaulted out of my penthouse and was on the street in seconds to help repack. So impressed with my Good Samaritan service, she handed me a brand new 50 pence piece. Precious that currency was in our flat!

Sunday was my favourite day of the week; roast dinner round my girlfriend parents a welcome rest bite. Logan's tribe lived in Edinburgh. When I got home, sometimes we both took a walk to the 'Town House' for a pint and a natter. The electricity metres ate 50 pence pieces at an alarming rate, so to conserve cash, we often sat in the kitchen chatting, smoking and drinking too much coffee.

Logan and I adored The Beatles, but he was a musical purest who could not fathom my love of modern dance music. One day he brought in a huge chocolate cake, to celebrate his 26th birthday. We polished off the lot and had a few giggles and only later did I find out the full list of ingredients. Keith accused the other fellows of drugging him. There were a few skirmishes, but hey, we were young.

West Germany beat England in the World Cup Semi-Final that summer and in the evening I sat in my room alone in thought. The lads who shared the flat disliked football and everybody was out of rectangle silver pieces to feed Rita the Metre. No place for a depressed footy supporter, a black blanket enveloped my spirit as a thin strip of light filtered under the door.

Police sirens raged and drunken Englishmen roared Second World War chants. Grown men should have known better. Science Fiction a pure fantasy written by dreamers and I was one, imagine if humanity united against an alien threat in an apocalyptic 2020. God made us fresh blood and bone, regardless of what creed we are, and team we follow.

Once I had paid for rent and food, I did not have much money left to spend. When the government imposed the poll tax in England, saving became harder, placing me in a dilemma. I discovered how easy it was to fall into a spiral of despair. The landlord, religious, preached the gospel to us sinners, and was not so forgiving when we did not stump up the cash. Hypocrite he was, and sympathetic men do not have to pray for our souls.

Peter, a fellow in his fifties, moved in before I left. He was a widow and had fallen on hard times. Often we met in the hall and he spoke well, appeared educated, and lent me several overdue library books. One of my particular favourites was 'War of the Worlds' by H. G. Wells, written in 1898.

Once I arrived home late, and discovered Pete sprawled at the bottom of the stairs passed out drunk. I presumed he was dead. James and I carried him upstairs to his room, which was spotless. Despite suffering alcoholism, he still had his pride. The next day he had no recollection of the events but quoted George Orwell to perfection. He had met him long ago, and why should he lie because in England what profit is there from truth? When I look back with anger, I wish I could have done more.

Whenever I see the movie Rocky, and the room he lived, I recall that bedsit. In the late summer of 1990, we bought our first house. Often I thought of Peter and knew at a young age that fate could pull the rug from under ones feet in an instant. I learnt more whilst on the ropes than when winning and for the rest of my life I celebrated the underdog.

After we wed, we honeymooned in Florida as the Space Shuttle Atlantis few over our heads to the sound of Nat King Cole. It is the truth and not a quote I stole, and for now, we were on a roll. I played sport and ate well and the London Marathon became my goal.

Ipswich Town were no longer a force, now languishing in the second tier of English football. I had not been to Portman Road in a while. When I settled with a new life, I ventured back, and chewed the fat with mates, singing and chanting as if it were a decade earlier. Yet, times had changed since the tragic events at Hillsborough.

The 1991/92 season was the last before the terraces disappeared. John Wark was the only survivor from the glory days and I attended every game. The Blues had won the league when Brighton Hove Albion came to visit on a glorious summer afternoon. Party time, the ground rocked, and at the final whistle we ran on and carried players shoulder high off the green grass of home.

The following year I joined a local football team. Real pie and chips, Sunday league stuff. Half the blokes had had better days and many suffered hangovers. Spectators where few, and once, one man and his dog made fun of our performance. Frustrated at the abuse, a teammate took the ball and blasted it at the old boy from a few feet out to send him flying. Unfortunately, his Alsatian chased everyone round the pitch, in a spectacle that was terrifying, albeit comic.

Walberswick is 40 miles away in the wilds of Suffolk. Goodness knows why they were in our league. The playing surface was on the heathland. Eight of our team started the fixture, because four players together in one car were half an hour late. Akin to Rorke's Drift, we defended keeping the score a draw until the troops arrived.

Often we had no match officials and once a passing stranger volunteered. We enjoyed a fine performance before he noticed we had 12 men on the field. Zippy the Captain reminded him we only had 10 the week beforehand. Disillusioned, he ended the debacle five minutes early to get home for Sunday Roast, followed by a hail of abuse.

Twiggy the goalkeeper was a ladies' man. We dubbed him that because of his size. During one game, two female spectators distracted him. At first, the pair appeared to be getting on okay until they attacked our lothario teammate who had been dating both girls. Lambs to the slaughter as our keeper sort refuge in his car, several players took turns in between the posts with comic consequences.

Athletic, for a hefty person, he must have been an acrobat in younger days. Twigs dived for lost causes and made the art of goalkeeping look effortless. Without him the following weekend, we had a cup game and nobody wished to go in goal. I volunteered. Whilst wearing a smelly green jersey and worn out gloves, experts briefed me on the rules. These were desperate times.

The manager did not want me to take kicks as he had a beast who could boot a football the full length of the field. Six leagues above, the opposition looked the business. When the game began, most of the play was in our half. The match developed into an unrelenting onslaught, and in a quarter of an hour, we were trailing by five goals.

At the interval, I feared a rollicking, but nobody wanted to be in my position. I glanced at our team sweating on a chilly winter's day. A few puffed on cigarettes as the opposition practised free kicks with the nonchalance of kings. Billy Wallace Gromit, our manager, had a cunning plan. Defend deep. He bore no resemblance to the legendary Scottish warrior, but he was a Scot and looked similar to a chap in the clever cartoon series.

That morning I was proud of the blokes that chased every ball after the interval. Late in the game, a wanderer turned on a sixpence and hit a 30-yard bullet. The thunderbolt bent my hand back, broke my fingers and smacked me in the face before sailing over the bar. Okay, we lost, but with brave hearts, my team had restored pride. The Beast, pumped full of adrenaline, did a celebratory Klinsmann dive after the final whistle and slid through dog poop. A fitting end, as we were the proverbial.

The tiny terrace house we lived was our palace. The neighbours were a retired couple, old enough to be our grandparents, and we spoke daily in the back garden. Coronation Street vibes of times gone by, it was easy to chat with a neighbour several doors up the road. Bob the lad opposite was a builder. I had just started playing squash and bumped into him often at the Holly's Sports and Social Club in Foxhall. Soon we teamed up for regular matches and a few pints, the dominant left hand giving me an advantageous spitfire serve.

On one occasion, when we could only book a late court, we had several beers beforehand. That was an interesting game for sure, shooting our coordination to smithereens. That said we sobered up good before we returned home. We had to grow up fast and build a life for our families, which was something worth living for as we held out for tomorrow.

Bob and I were both 26 by 1994, and we knew responsibility was closing in, and within a year we were fathers and a new chapter and verse was to begin. The maze of existence strewn with triumph and failure is a dress rehearsal for fatherhood. Another human dependent on your maturity is life changing. We had seen things they could never see, and yes, now no longer in a blur, but an oasis of joy!

Marathon of Faith

Mile 11

'I'm not a monarchist. But I'm English. And I have
an irrational emotion for my country.'

Damon Albarn

Autumn 1995 during my wife's pregnancy, I was
full of apprehension. Once again, angst and self-doubt
raged. When worried I prayed as a kid. Howbeit, I
have never regarded myself religious. Therefore, I
drove to the local cemetery where it was quiet, and I
could ponder. A bright new era dawning, the song
Eleanor Rigby by The Beatles, reverberated as if a
wasp spinning in my brain despite not recalling the
classic lyrics in their entirety.

Amongst the stones and trees, I stared around, waiting
for Father McKenzie to lead the way. The heavens
opened, and water tumbled from the sky. Frozen in
time for a minute, the eyes stung, listening to nature's
flow, before sauntering back to the car soaked to the
skin. Now, protected from the elements, I rubbed my
face, dried my hair with my sleeve, and sneezed.

Cigarette in mouth, I looked out of the window, and
lit up as the brief, but heavy shower slowly
disappeared into a silence to reveal a blue suburban

sky. The sunlight shone brightly and a spectrum of colours curved over the horizon as I squinted through half-closed eyes. The sun and the rain had washed away my weariness and fear, as birds sang in a melody of optimism.

Wipers on to clear the view, a smudge had appeared on the windscreen in the shape of a large cross and a robin redbreast rested on the bonnet. Logic explains, but an angel had shown me the way. For we have evolved over millions of years full of faith, hope and belief. Man can fly to the moon. However, who gave humanity the mind to think and the tools to build, in a rich open field of treasure.

The moment I became a parent lingers with me eternally. Overwhelming responsibility washed over me as we left the ward with my son and tenderly placed him on to the back seat of our car. Transition from boy to man passed in an instant. I wanted to be a great dad!

No one can survive alone and we need each other whether it is family, friends or the kindness of a passing stranger. The National Lottery had started and people thought 'hey, tomorrow might just be my lucky day'. I never bothered with buying a ticket, because happiness was never about money, although it takes the sting out of poverty. Only love, the air that we breathe, and life God gives is free. For no wealth brings genuine joy.

We arrived home on our little street where dustbin lids pointed to the sky to pull in moving pictures from the stars. We opened the front door, switched on the light in the hall and walked into the living room. I placed my lad on the floor still in his stroller and switched on the TV. As we sat on the couch and hugged, the band Blur appear on the screen dressed in white as Damian Albarn stared out of the box to say we made it. The universal was here, although I no longer wore the gear. Fashion was a luxury. Problems left alone, weekends were our own.

The roads we walked were on air, and as I looked at my wife, I wondered how we got there. Life was too perfect. Every new generation replaces the old. I had done nothing with the cards fate dealt me and I was already 27. Endlessly I would sit with my lad as he slept on my lap, as I pontificated about the world he had arrived. I was tipping him the wink and giving him a head start, for he would be a better man than I.

By 1996, I sought activities more suitable for family living. I even built a gym in the shed at the bottom of the garden so I could be home more often. Huge iron weight and bars I bought from a mate for 25 quid and a bench from MFI. Tape cassette loaded with Rocky, the soundtrack inspired. I bored with it soon, but the competitiveness of squash I still enjoyed.

In one particular match, I picked up a nasty injury. I am left-handed, a confusable advantage and dangerous. A mirror image of our opponents, everything we do is back to front. On this day, Buster the Windmill swung his arm to smash the ball into the wall. We called him that because of his unorthodox action. The racket thumped into my face as I felt the metallic taste. Bloody and dazed, I wanted to carry on as I was winning.

Windy Miller was having none of it and retired white as a sheet. Hells bells, it must be bad. Game abandoned, we returned to the changing room where I could see the damage caused. The middle of my nose was split and in an awful mess. Oh well, I got a free match out of it. No way would he take my money. I should have gone to hospital to have stitches but went home and taped it up as best I could.

For weeks, I wore a plaster, and at my son's christening, I looked as if I had been boxing. It disappointed me I now had a large scar on my nose and was self-conscious of the fact. Dad suggested it gave me character and not to worry. However, those words are easy without the mirror, as the visual reminder.

Three months after the injury, I visited the doctors to see what they could do. I know Ipswich is a relatively small town, but waiting in reception with me was Windy Miller, the perpetrator. He recognised me, but we did not speak, as he was the last person I wanted to meet. The doctor was flippant, but we had a good chat.

Before I left, I mentioned the coincidence of how his last patient was the guy who inflicted the injury. Doc nodded and raised an eyebrow and for a while, we discuss the unexplainable. Science a tool, a man who ignores instinct is a fool. Perhaps the visit fated, and the faded scar I see today a reminder of life's journey.

On one occasion, I booked a court, and Alex the Mate let me down. So, I went outside for a jog. The run I relished so much, frequently I headed out into the countryside instead of booking a game. Often, if mates played a match on a Saturday, I met them later in the clubhouse for a quick pint. Around this time, someone set a gym up where I worked. Until this point, I had avoided those places. Gyms were for bodybuilders, I thought. Before each session, I warmed up on the treadmill.

Cool Britannia and the sixties were in vogue. For years, I had appreciated the harmony of the Beatles. Free as a bird, they returned once again with a little help from Mr Blue Sky. Yes, I was a youth of the eighties but it was apparent I was not the only one inspired by the melody of Lennon, McCartney and George, as Brit Pop stormed the music charts with a sound that was familiar yet modern and relevant.

However, I could not get used to the birth of lad culture. I was a husband and father with a mortgage while men a decade older than I made the country laugh by behaving badly, and some wore football shirts as fashion items. It was as if the instant I stepped forwards the world took a step backward. Footy came home briefly and inevitably we lost to the Germans once again in an almost Shakespearian tragedy.

Days later, I was at Hyde Park in London to watch The Who as Saint George flags fluttered in the wind. This was a celebration of British culture, and my last chance to see them, or so I thought. The atmosphere was electric before the internet and social media changed how we related to one another.

The festival was a mass gathering of the common people. Without phones, we arranged where to meet up if we disappeared into a sea of humanity. For this was the Quadrophenia Tour. The operatic angst helped me through teenage years, when I was a slave to phoney leaders who pounded the stage like clowns with bouffant hair and hollow speeches.

The spitfire flies over Beachy Head to the colours of blue, white and red, and on that day, I memorised every word that Townshend wrote and Daltrey screamed and said. They were not causing a big sensation; they merely spoke for 'my' generation.

Tony Blair and New Labour won the General Election in 1997 and we moved house. Sunday the 31st of August was the usual routine as I had a squash match. When I got up, I heard a car crash had killed the Princess of Wales. There was a sick feeling in my stomach and although not a royalist, I liked her. The entire country let go of the stiff upper lip in a torrent of pent-up tears. She had suffered Bulimia and for the first time I told my wife of my experience a decade beforehand.

I met Lady Di many years earlier when she came to visit Ipswich. I stood in silence as she shook folk's hands, taken aback by how natural she looked. She could have been the girl next door thrown into a fantasy world of kings, queens and duty. I remember that face frozen in time and think anonymity is the dream, because cloud cuckoo land must be a crushing disappointment. Everybody has 15 minutes of fame and I am sure I have had mine, thank the lord.

Life is too short. I chatted to Sandy, who attended my local gym a few days later. We discussed the royals, and I asked if he had ever considered entering the London Marathon as we talked next to each other on the treadmill. I suppose it was as if I was running out of time.

Thirty, approached. My pal ran further than I did, and I guessed he was faster. Interested, he suggested entering the Felixstowe Half Marathon in October. Blimey six weeks to train, that is a blink of an eye. If this book were a film, the theme tune to the Stanley Kubrick space extravaganza would play as my story took a twist in the trail.

I began training, albeit on the gym's hamster wheel. I huffed, and I puffed as time crept slowly listening to music to help pass the miles. The two debut albums by Oasis were eight minutes shy of an hour and that is how long I ran. I was a changing man, built on shifting sand.

I needed a masterplan, because you can search for a lifetime dancing in the sunshine to find something worth striving for. Yet, I could be no one else, only myself and although I desired to write, I had not lived. So still young, I would push physically until the brain learnt more while the body wore.

On the day of the event, most of my family converged on the east coast to watch me attempt the challenge I had dismissed as a piece of cake. The reality was profoundly different. Fifty minutes toiling away on a running machine listening to the dulcet tones of Liam Gallagher was not an ideal preparation. The longest run had been seven slow miles. This race would definitely wear out two Oasis albums and maybe more, and I was yet to buy an iPod. The backing track would be the wind, the sea and the sound of pain.

I had the gear, comprising a vest, shorts and a pair of cheap glinting white trainers I bought at Tesco. Gordon Bennett, I was in for a rough ride, and he would not help when the going got tough. Sandy looked fit and had run the distance several times in the previous few weeks. Good luck pal and see you on Monday. He would not hang about waiting for me, as I had more support than most local running clubs did.

Failure the mother of success, the event was two-laps, and I showboated and waved to the family along the seafront before whipping round once again. The next was much harder, as I had run further than I ever had. Runners overtook in droves as I slowed at mile nine, lacking stamina. Everything a learning curve, I resolved not to make that mistake again.

The race was sheer agony and a humbling experience. Although I felt embarrassed at finishing near the back of the field, I had a sense of accomplishment and picked up a medal I did not think I merited. The adventure could have ended there. However, everybody appeared cheerful, and there was a genuine community spirit.

Running made me feel better and races were a family day out. In later years, my children enjoyed the fun runs. There were few in those days. The seaside jaunt transformed my life. Eventually I bettered my time by half an hour. What appealed was it was not a team sport. Ideal for shift work, I trained when I choose.

Others might disagree when I claim it is an individual pursuit. Every race, I try to improve and make it best I can in this world, as a husband, father, son and a postie. Phew, I kept that quiet, having worked for Royal Mail since I was 20. For I am a face in the crowd, the commentators mention on The Mall in London. The club athlete some call fun runners, attempting to run under 3 hours 30 minutes. That time always sounded an excellent target.

Sometimes running has been too important. Addiction lurks in the most positive pursuit. That said, taking up the sport was life changing, clearing the brain of poison in thought. Cigarettes I quit, which was a logical and seamless progression. It seemed ridiculous to fill the lungs with smoke after a workout.

Sandy and I were unsuccessful through the ballot system in 1998, and he gave up and never raced again. Undeterred, I continued entering races throughout Suffolk, Essex and Norfolk and eventually got a place in 1999. Around the same time, my better half announced she was pregnant.

If ever you wait for the perfect date, it never arrives. When the opportunity comes to join 30,000 on the streets of the capital, take it. Sport is a metaphor for life. Sylvester Stallone used this to significant effect in the movie Rocky, an everyman story of a guy who just wanted to go the distance. Inspired in part by this, London was calling. The anticipation was palpable and a daunting prospect. Proper training would start in the New Year in unknown territory and fear of the dreaded wall.

Felixstowe Road Runners enquired if I wanted to join, as I was not a member of a club. Greg, a workmate and fellow runner, said it was a wonderful idea, and the experience would help. The following Tuesday evening he joined me for a drive to the coast to check them out.

When we arrived, we found the members were an amiable crowd. Runners of similar ability paired off into groups. Once we found a bunch of guys and girls we thought we could keep up with, off we trotted. The veterans knew their stuff, and it was a pleasant change to run along the seafront. Afterwards, we joined three of the chaps for a drink and hung on their every word as they spoke of The London Marathon.

One tale lingers in my mind. Steve, a seasoned runner, said he became confused at around 23 miles when he spotted a sign saying Kerbs, he thought read Kurds. For a moment, he assumed he was in Turkey. A strange story, but years later I ran into the mental and physical barrier. Positivity is a fool without proper preparation.

The evening was great, but the next week we gave our local Ipswich club a go. Jaffa for short, their full name is 'Jogging and fitness for all'. When we turned up, we stood out like sore thumbs and looked ready for a five-a-side footy match. Inspired, we joined and soon got into a routine.

London was the only marathon for me, but now a veteran of hundreds of events I have a more rounded perspective. Gradually I morphed into a runner akin to the pictures of the evolution of man. Running became a habit, and when fitter, my confidence grew. The journey to the start line had twisted and turned. Whatever route destiny had mapped, all roads would lead to Blackheath, Greenwich on a cold and wet spring in April...

London Marathon

'Avoiding pain is not a capacity of survival, but an excuse to avoid living.'

Mark Lankester

On a chilly January morn, training for the 20th century's final London Marathon began as Greg and I met with a group of like-minded dudes. Amazed we were to embark on a 12 miler, I expected to build up somewhat and harboured concerns over the distance. Heck, I never spoke up, as I was the interloper.

Bruce a forty something was the team leader and most runners appeared to be older. I felt young in comparison, as most of my peers still played footy and ran to shed a few pounds in pre-season. The marathoners we headed out with had done it all and Willis, a tall lad, wore a white cotton tee shirt from the Ipswich Marathon of 1983. I remember being somewhat impressed by that.

The run went smoothly as I listened with interest to breathless voices, but after seven miles, the pack picked up the pace, and for once, I had little to say. Out of the comfort zone, I drifted on, and then bailed out in sight of home. Blimey, my pal and I had better shape up or ship out.

The snippets of information I heard that morning nailed themselves into the brain as if post-it notes. They agreed the 20-mile mark is the halfway stage and a 10k after that is a momentous task. Energy conservation is vital while thumping your weary legs against concrete for hours. For whether you stride eastward or west, the trail is unforgiving.

God did not design the human to run marathons. Imagine your fuel supply as a jug of water. Tip up too far and fast and it will not last long. The elastic band, when supple, will stretch and expand, yet the snap is painful on one's hand. The body is the tool, and to abuse it makes a fool. On any given day the inches we need are within us all, one step at a time until we see that chink of light and lift ourselves up on one's road to destiny.

The following Sunday, we returned better rested in the right gear. I carried so much water Carol nicknamed me Gunga Din. Later, I looked up the character. Oh dear, he died, albeit heroically. Kipling I find inspiring. The writer, not the king of cakes, I must add, although they are not bad.

Yep, the eleven miles was tough, but we gritted teeth with a dose of determination. Greg was not running at London and stopped tagging along as the distances increased. Each weekend from then on, I headed out, alone at my pace. Howbeit I still ran a mid-week 10 miler on club nights.

Kirton near Felixstowe, my favourite long run, I measured by car. The village name derived from the Anglo-Saxon word 'Kirtatuna' that means church town. There and back, routes are easier to measure, but cross-country runs became pure guesswork before GPS watches.

Later on in this tale, I talk in added detail of my second London Marathon. The recollections are clearer, as I recorded the experience on paper. In hindsight, the adventure of 1999 was a dress rehearsal, the mock exam and reconnaissance mission for the future.

I recall around that time, the Football Association sacked England's manager, Mr Diamond Lights, after remarks made as regards to the disabled. I hoped journalists had taken those words out of context. The FA called up a superstar to replace Glenn. Kevin Keegan had been on Top of the Pops more than the Spurs legend. He could sing, inspire and was head over heels in love with England.

The long training runs a voyage of discovery, it was not so much what I learned, but how I changed. Boredom never a problem as the miles and time on my feet increased, I felt lost in total tranquillity as the senses became sharper. Colours brighter, sounds clearer, the rustle of leaves, the crunch of snow and even the vehicles on the road danced a hypnotic hum.

The treadmill I used on occasions, but it took so much energy to stay in one place. We humans strive so hard to keep the status quo and root our lives in a spot we call home. The world is a beauty we only see in its

131

entirety if we keep in perpetual motion. As I write these words, I have not run on the conveyor belt of fitness in months, and have yet to slip. The journey of nothingness can crush the spirit, as if in a hamster's wheel where nothing is real, because the fields and trails I trod live forever.

Mid-March, Ipswich Jaffa put on a bus to the Reading Half Marathon, and a Suffolk tribe descended on Berkshire along with 6000 other runners. The event had a fantastic atmosphere. The experience helped, as I had never run a big race. A few famous faces were there, including Sally Gunnell, who took the warm-up whilst encouraging the crowd.

Neil Webb, the ex-England international footballer, had entered. Smiler was only 35 years old. Whenever I saw the lad on the TV, he always appeared so happy. Later in life, I discovered that looks and behaviour could be deceptive. I am not talking of Webby in particular. Nevertheless, when his career ended, he did struggle to adjust. The course a buzz, I finished in 1:49. Afterwards, we visited the pub and had a few beers. It surprised me how many runners enjoyed alcohol, and few drank orange. Soon I was Jafferised!

The following week I asked Dad if he wished to come along on his bike for a half marathon. If I could run, he was sure he could peddle. Sunday morning he rode the two miles to my house on his ancient boneshaker, with a flask full of coffee, and off we headed uphill towards Kirton. Every time my father shifted gear, the antique clonked and squeaked. I noticed he wore cycle clips, and I remembered how I used them to stop tripping over my flared trousers whilst playing football on Maxie Fields. A memory forgotten, I smiled inside.

My training back then looks little more than an average runner's weekly mileage. The bulk of which was at weekends. Six days as a postie with a toddler and a pregnant wife, my running was not life, instead an infinitesimal part of a bigger picture. When I finished working out, it was never a case of feet up, a kip or a video. Often we went to the park to entertain our young son. I am not making excuses or complaining. In fact, now my children have grown up I miss those times.

The diehards said three runs a week were insufficient. Well, whatever Bruce and Willis claimed, I knew how much energy I had to give. Roger Bannister suggested life is a balance. He did not do so shabbily, although I am not comparing my foray into running, only the message. Today, I would not take on the distance with such scant preparation. Back then, the road ahead was uncharted. Still a smoker, I quit gaining a chewing habit that lasts to this day.

While at Jaffa, I hooked up with cousin Vinny, who had a marathon place. By March, I had built up a solid base and asked him to join me for a 15 miler. I was the Route Master who knew Ipswich, or so I thought. Blood is thicker than water, but he did not know how thick I was. Pre Sat Nav I could get lost in a lift and halfway, I took a wrong turn. We ended up running 19, and he was livid. He laughed months later, and for an unknown reason refused to accompany me on my final long run!

Twenty years have since passed, and I have had many adventures. Howbeit, I never regarded myself as a true runner, just a bloke hoping to finish. London is a monumental event I craved to be part of, and that was the motivation. When I began, I needed inspiration from others more accomplished. During training, I dropped weight, and stamina increased. Astonished how much mileage I could do if required. One run lingers long in the mind.

In early April, I met up again with a few characters from the club, for an 18 miler. We headed towards Melton near Woodbridge as I hung on their every word. Yet the moment we were at mile 14, I realised I was in trouble trekking cross-country. Snow fell, and I was the only person in the group wearing shorts with no hat and gloves. Shirtsleeves over hands, I told the gang I was taking a shortcut to Ipswich and zigzagged through the countryside to emerge in Martlesham. The muddy fields were troublesome, and the uneven surface aggravated an old back injury. Today I run that distance on a whim.

The route was further than I thought, as an inner voice guided me forward. A brick bus shelter looked enticing, but I pushed on as motorists drove past, oblivious to my pain. Never did I stop, and in just under three hours, I arrived home to the smell of roast dinner and warmth. Lewis, who I got on with well, rang my wife to see if I was okay. I once saw him drink from a puddle to avoid dehydration. True, I was flaky, but my pal was as mad as a hatter. As she talked to him, I staggered in to announce I had run 20 miles.

Now as I look through the looking glass, I remember the unplanned escapade equipped my soul, and I was upbeat from that moment. Yet, within the hour, once again on kiddie patrol, I was building a snowman. Afterwards, I had a bath. Whilst soothing my aching legs, an interview with David Bowie came on the radio, and I got interested. Dave said the Internet was to transform our lives. I thought he was exaggerating, as I did not have a computer. The Starman had a crystal ball. He was no fool.

The night before the marathon, I checked out the Rocky movie between reading to my son and flicking through Pokémon cards. I watched so many kids TV shows in those days, such as Bob the builder and Thomas the Tank Engine. The Sylvester Stallone flick shone biblically in comparison, and the inspiration gave me heart on the roads of the capital. I was dreaming when I wrote this so forgive me if I go astray, but when I awoke, I knew it to be judgement day.

April 18th, 1999, the morning of the race, the Jaffa bus was to depart Northgate Sports Centre at six o'clock sharp. While I sorted my kitbag, I mulled over what drove thousands of individuals to get out of their beds on a Sunday to conquer 26.2 miles. The London Marathon shines in the British psyche to depict something tough, but not beyond reach, and is part of our vocabulary. Chris Brasher, co-founder of the event, dubbed it the Suburban Everest. I interpret those words to mean a calling that will test the human spirit.

My family travelled to the capital with me. On the coach, I detected a few big day haircuts. The minute I sat down, I ate sandwiches, crisps and pizza. We showed up at Blackheath in excellent time. They used it as a burial pit for Londoners who perished in the great plague of 1665 and it was where King Henry VII defeated Cornish rebels. The feud was over taxation. Things never change!

Family and friends took photos before runners and spectators separated. A brisk spring morning, I wore a vest and an old tee shirt I could throw away when warmed up after a few miles. I did not expect to freeze to death in April. Training is not only fitness but also preparation. Cool running whilst above three degrees Celsius, I learnt I felt much warmer when on the run.

When I trained, I suffered chafing, so I used Vaseline in problematic areas. The little details are crucial in big races, the longer on one's feet. Do not forget to trim your toenails a few days before, unless you want the discomfort of bloody toes. One item I forgot was a spare pair of shoelaces.

My cousin joined me on the common. Wombling free, we observed other runners preparing in their own way. Vinny's face reflected my fear, and to put him at ease, I said that, at least we would not get lost today. He grinned, remembering our last outing. Throughout marathon training, he had back problems.

We had agreed to run together. However, I was in pen three, and he was in six. Because of his injury, he expected to be slower.

To relax, we laughed, recalling childhood memories, whilst a sea of people swam around us in waves. Some looked timid and others primed for action. Everybody was in their own world, and I sensed the air of tension. I saw Chris Chittell and Edward Peel from the soap Emmerdale and smiled in their direction as if they were friends. Blimey, fame must be loathsome.

We queued forever at the toilets. Once we had transferred our bags on to the baggage truck, we wandered to the start. Vince had a phone with him and a bum bag. Back then, I never contemplated getting a mobile let alone running with one. The only technology I had was a cheap Casio watch. With no drink or energy gels, I wondered what lay ahead. Disaster struck as I snapped a shoelace, but a Good Samaritan had a spare.

There were two alternative start points at Greenwich and St Johns Park. We started at Blackheath, Shooters Hill Road. The three starts merged at 5k. Each had nine pens, number one being the fastest. Eager to join the third corral, my cousin insisted he was staying in six. Sure, I could break sub four hours, I was sceptical, but in the want of moral support, I agreed.

In the days before chip timing, the race started when the klaxon sounded. Our running club told us to start our watches as we stepped over and to stop them at the finish. For, Ipswich Jaffa officials accepted watch times regardless of the results in the newspaper.

Tower Bridge near halfway is where I hoped to see family. Afterwards, I planned to meet them at Trafalgar Square. With no mobile, heaven knows what would have happened if I had become injured or lost. Homing pigeons could have been a valiant plan, as there were plenty pestering Nelson.

The horn sounded, and nobody moved. Restless, I turned to Vinny, who looked far too relaxed, and I feared I had made a mistake. A quarter of an hour later, we edged forwards with the tide. Heck, the elites had covered three miles. So now frozen with a heavy heart I had time to dwell.

My wife was six months pregnant, and I worried for her and our unborn child. When we crossed the start line, I knew to run less than four hours was to be a tall order. When I started my watch, we still walked. I spotted my family early and lost Vince in the stampede of rhinos, centipedes, and pantomime horses.

The Cutty Sark Ship at 10k was to witness a massive bottleneck. Dad called out, and the sound of his voice lifted the spirits. Thousands of joyful faces lined the pavements, a dozen deep in places, handing out an abundance of food. Children stood with unwrapped sweets, and I ate the starbursts to fuel my stride.

At around mile 10, a market trader shouted apples and hurled the fruit high above our heads. I reached out with one hand to a rhapsody of the Queens Subjects approval. The ovation was for him and the thousands who lined the streets. The chill in the air and light drizzle ideal for running, I hoped to see my folks halfway.

Tower Bridge extraordinary, I knew it was now real and kept glancing to the left, disappointed not to see family. Nevertheless, with official photographers aplenty, 20 years on a visual reminder rests on the mantelpiece. Once, I replaced it with a modern picture, but my daughter became upset, as it had been there her entire life. Hence, today I remain frozen in time crossing the Thames.

The trouble with shorts is chaffing. Lycra I wore in training and never had an issue, so used them on the day. Howbeit, if they had ripped, I had no underwear underneath. The dubious fashion discarded in a bin in Trafalgar Square post-race, a relic of the 20th century . The wolf whistles from the crowd, not for me, were for a celebrity gladiator from the popular television show sporting similar attire.

At 14 and 21 miles, the routes pass each other. As I tired and the pain set in, faster runners flew past in the opposite direction. Cones divided the road, or more likely metal barriers as the high buildings of Canary Wharf shut out the sun. My father-in-law worked there and collected the race number for me during the week to save me the special trip.

The sky a purple haze, the Blackfriars underpass loomed. Strange happenings occurred on entering the artificial light. The real marathon appeared, folks relaxing where no cameras lurked to film the pain.

Imagine the backstage of a concert before the band rushes out. Runners sought to compose themselves before emerging into the sunlight and a clown leant against the wall in tears.

Adrenaline on the wane, I staggered until a woman slapped me hard on the shoulder and told me to keep running. It stung, but I appreciated the motivational battering. A few minutes later six police officers I remembered from the Reading Half Marathon dressed in custodian helmets and wielding truncheons, surrounded me. Unique sights of a peoples race rich in British eccentricity.

Once, when we were kids, Dad on night shift, Mum took my sister and I on a short train ride to London during the school holidays. When I spotted the beefeaters and the ravens, I shouted that I could see the bloody tower. Horrified, she told me not to swear, so I chanted the phrase repeatedly. To be honest, I knew what I was doing, and tis a personality trait I never lost.

Two decades later, running past the famous castle that once imprisoned the Krays, my punishment awaited. The cobbles were at the 23-mile point where a green mat lay to make the passage smoother for tiring feet. Although a horrible hurdle, the space on the outside of carpeted stones gave me the opportunity to pass people. For once again, a laminated photo recorded ones pain, of number 9729 striving through rain.

The Clock Tower in sight, Big Ben chimed a broken sound that rang through the city Boudica burnt to the ground. There is so much beauty in imperfection. The bell that is the heartbeat of London has a hole in it, never properly repaired, giving a slightly distorted tone. For this race was not to be perfection as my watch rapidly approached four hours with a mile left to run. Yet I did not care and felt a sense of savoir-faire.

The spin into The Mall, glorious, the end in sight, I lifted my arms early to finish in 4:10:14. Determined to beat the time on another date, I logged the pitfalls to draw on if I ever had a second chance. After I picked up my medal, I strolled to see Nelson and the clan and whilst snagging a smoke I avoided the cameraman.

Everything I tell in this book is true, although I changed people's names and that could be you. Reality dawned when I met my wife at Trafalgar square, her hug better than the Norwich City coloured ribboned medallion I dared to wear. More than a race, the London Marathon is a charity and I ran for Macmillan Cancer Support, folk's generosity amazing.

Disappointed not to be fleet of foot, regrets emerged once adrenaline had worn. Seven years later, I would be back for the sequel, fitter, leaner and stronger, aiming to break 3:30. Thirty Thousand souls had taken part for the first time in the race's history. Sat in my armchair that evening drinking coffee watching TV highlights, the day's events were a blur. I could not believe that a few hours earlier a Tractor Boy had been one of a cast of shuffling feet, and never once did I contemplate defeat.

Millennium

Mile 13

'Time was on my side with no place left to hide.'

Mark Lankester

Stars direct faith, and one shimmers above St Augustine's Church near home as nightfall descends. The cross lit with neon hangs in the sky as if alone, with no building below to hold the glow. Star Trek I watched as a kid and the 21st century I looked forward to with anticipation. The future often portrayed as an undesirable place in popular culture, I speculated what world waited once I reached thirty something.

Okay, the millennium was nigh. The dome built, as was the London Eye. So, without missing a trick, I purchased a Nokia brick. The weight I was to carry, too big for the pockets of a mobile man. The phone lasted 15 years. Minus grey hairs, lines of time, and aching limbs, I was at my physical peak in the dawn of the second millennia.

Hot July brings blooming flowers, pollinated by buzzing bees while the sun shines brightly and I hope for ice cool showers. Tis a pretty month of year when girls wear summer dresses, and weather fine we forget some of those stresses.

Yes, I am man and boy at heart. I admit I know little of the workings of the female of the species. Talking to like-minded blokes is easy, tuned into the same station, with a knowing glance and few words. A man-child stays locked in a world of childlike nonsense and pontification.

Mark, you are a dad once more. Congratulations, a baby girl. Wow, I held her in my arms as if a delicate flower. I noticed her jet-black hair and large brown eyes that were the same as mine. Perhaps a cowardly statement, but raw, genuine emotion is tough, and I feared bursting into tears in front of the nurses.

When happy every day is summer. I marvelled at her first steps. Often we drove to Christchurch Park to feed the ducks when alone. If we did not make the pond at the bottom of the hill, I paused as she stared at the birds and the elegance of nature. I wondered what thoughts flickered looking into my face, not so soft and warm. My voice deep, I fretted the tone would strike fear.

Instead of repeating boring anecdotes, I sang renditions of The King. One particular favourite was 'Young and Beautiful', and when I thought of giving up, further ballads would rise from my coffee cup, as she fell into slumber after yet another Elvis number. When I think of those times, the theme that truly narrates my emotion has no words. For a baby has none, the classic 'Nimrod' by Edward Elgar capturing the vibe.

May 2000, I visited London to witness the Tractor Boys return to the top flight of English football. The famous Twin Towers framed the stadium as if a Roman Amphitheatre. Strange, the Colosseum in Rome has stood for centuries, yet the old Wembley survived less than 80. Buildings come and go sometimes faster than we grow.

On August 22nd, a bronze statue of Sir Alf Ramsey rose outside Ipswich Town FC. I remembered walking past the majestic man's house as a small child and Mum saying he won The Blues the league and England the World Cup. Those words fresh in mind, I took a walk to the ground with my daughter, with a scarf tucked in pram.

I repeated those same comments as she gazed up at the sculpture, before placing the neck warmer on the plinth below Alfie's feet. A smile lit up her face, as if understanding the language I muttered. Never too far do I roam on the Suffolk streets I call home. Ambition Mark you have none, yet as my running form improved I had so much fun.

The year 2001 was to be no race odyssey. Foot and Mouth broke out and swept the nation as farmers fought to control the epidemic. There was a risk of contamination between farms if people carried the virus on shoes and hands. Therefore, authorities restricted movement in the countryside, making training difficult with areas covered in barbed wire.

An eccentric old boy lived on one of my rural runs. I still see him today and we are on friendly terms. In fact, Mr Stevens is a tremendous musician and such people always impress. Often he chatted and trotted beside me as I went past his house. He acted that way with everybody, and I choose an alternative route when timing a run.

When Suffolk Radio broke the news, he charged out to yell that I was the spreader of disease. Please go away. Mr Hurdy-Gundy could play a tune for sure but squawked. Obstacle out manoeuvred, I gained momentum, heading towards a taped off footpath and leapt to freedom. Although impressed with my hurdling ability, I pulled a muscle.

Stop that man! He must have woken half the neighbourhood and I waved, retreating into woodland. No more signs, I saw runners, hikers and dog walkers, one of whom was former Ipswich Town manager Bobby Ferguson. Soon I realised my nemesis had cordoned off the path, and I felt less guilt.

Suffolk rural, the virus decimated local road running calendars. Small races vanished, never to return. The Brantham 5 disappeared for seven years. Before the Internet, I hunted for events in the Runner's World Magazine. Unofficial runs popped up, a fiver to enter, with no results or medals during the restrictions.

Long before free parkrun's throughout the country, one of these was the Halstead 10k. Three hundred entrants turned up just glad to run and queued for a piece of paper with a number written in pen. The race started at a traffic cone. There were no marshals on the course, I took a wrong turn and not alone, a few runners made a gargantuan mistake by following my lead.

Sure, it is easy to take nature for granted in Suffolk, living minutes from open fields. Lost many a time running in the town I love, it's an absurdity some think Ipswich a four-letter word. For a man sat by a freshwater spring complained he was thirsty. Water gives life, yet he could not see a shop in sight.

Once we stayed a week in the New Forest, one of the largest in England covering 150 square miles. Wild horses roamed to the delight of my baby girl. The wonder of discovery was heart-warming. The time I spent pointing to unfamiliar creatures, I realised how I was seeing the world through her eyes. So many souls switch off senses in adulthood and the far-reaching island I live on is a miracle to behold.

The caravan we stayed in was on the edge of the woodland. The first night I ran through the rustling trees that formed a cathartic experience amongst a sea of green. Howbeit, after a few miles it was a relief to discover a farmhouse and find I had not wandered too far from civilisation. Trouble is, after passing the rustic dwelling on at least four occasions, disorientated, I became lost.

IPod switched on to the music of The Beatles, the odd horse shook a head in dismay, and deer dashed across my path. Humans are a strange breed, Bronco might think. In harmony with my frame of mind, John Lennon sang of a walrus. Nonsense to nonbelievers, the chorus made perfect sense.

The Lewis Carroll poem must have inspired the song, and soon I sensed something wrong. Dehydration is the death knell to man, and in a riddle of rhythm I prayed for the sight of a watering can, and better still an ice-cream van.

Hungry and parched, a rose hip bush caught my eye, an edible wild berry common in the terrain during the summer. Bear Grylls in mind, I swallowed five. Paul McCartney's long winding road became annoying for obvious reasons, as I pulled the headphones from my ears. The woodland creepy as darkness loomed, invisible cries raised the hairs on one's neck, and off I fled.

Without a clue where I was, eight miles in a red blur darted through trees. The eerie movie 'Flatliners' came to mind. Help! The Scarlet Pimpernel was fast. Every time I glimpsed a darting flame, I yelled to attract the speed merchant's attention. The fella thereon put in a sprint that Carl Lewis would have been proud of and vanished. Gasping for breath, I spotted a dog walker and was near civilisation.

Mile 14, the caravan appeared. Later than planned, we ventured to the nearby clubhouse. On the way homeward, the lad and I had a kickabout, surrounded by the artificial lighting I take for granted. Rural England must have been a bleak place before The Police recorded synchronicity and the birth of electricity.

I noticed a chap sat on a wall, wearing running shoes whilst I did keepie-uppie. The natural icebreaker when meeting a lone ranger is football chat. Kev, a

Manchester United fan from Essex and I chewed the fat. I peered at his trainers before leaving and asked if he ran. Yes, he was a runner. A few hours earlier, he cut a training run short when hearing the yells of a crazy man.

April 27th 2002, I took the boy to his first ever-professional football match. Suffolk's finest were playing the Mancunian reds and international support, in the Premier League. Good seats secured high in the Cobbold Stand; we took a leisurely walk and mingled with the crowd. Supporters sang, the face of a child lit, and he became a fan for life whatever the clubs strife.

Not long after, he asked why I no longer played football. For, I was the same age as Paolo Maldini. True, an unfair comparison, but yes, he had a point. So I returned for a local team low in the league ladder, wanting the kid to have the same vague memories of me playing as I had of my dad who hung up his boots at 32.

Ten games played, Sonny Jim enjoyed the experience. Too young to appreciate the debacle, the characters intrigued the little man. On any given Sunday, we were as usual losing at half time. During the interval, we stood at the side of the pitch eating oranges, and a few puffed a smoke.

The club captain gave a Churchillian speech to lift the spirits. Pumped with adrenaline, we sprinted back yelling as if warriors, but within seconds were taken down with the sword of superiority.

On a bleak, wet February, the end was nigh. I wanted to score and finish on a high. Unexpectedly, a splendid opportunity presented. The ball sailed as a gift, with only the keeper to beat. Celebration planned, metres ahead of the defence, I could have rounded the goalkeeper. Shoot! Seconds later, I lay in mud after my shot sailed into the sky.

Sunday morning football for the second time was different. The opposition were younger. Most mates dropped off the radar. Family life, and less strenuous activities such as golf, appealed. Yet, occasionally, I detected a familiar face.

The last match of my illustrious career, an opposing player stood out with white hair. The old timer was either good, or they were short of players. Then, stepping forth, I recognised Stan. Too late to chat, we nodded before the ensuing battle.

The team did not look much, our mirror image. Armed with one sub, the manager would not risk taking off yours truly, because injuries were inevitable. Often in the low leagues, teams have a hand full of useful fellas who play on a Saturday and turn out Sunday for fun. If the ball fell to my feet, I passed to the pros and run.

I played in defence because a better man was unavailable. Stan in a similar role charged forwards continuously and ran over people like a Sherman tank. In self-preservation, I slid in with a poor tackle, and he somersaulted into the air and landed rolling in agony.

He should have had a round of applause for acting, or at least an equity card. Luckily, I avoided a red. Nonchalantly he threw the ball to a teammate who took the free kick and scored. Stan walked past and smiled. I fell for the ruse. When tired, he stumbled over frequently. He perfected the art of diving decades beforehand.

Post-match, Stanley and I stayed on the pitch and chatted. Before we left the field of broken dreams, he lamented that we had never escaped Maxie Fields and took a shot at goal from the halfway line. Unable to bend it like Beckham, the ball flew over the bar into a garden to the sound of breaking glass.

Bobby Moore and Alan Mullery appeared for Fulham in the FA Cup against West Ham in 1975 on the day of Frank's seventh birthday party. When walking off the Hallowed Turf together, both knew it to be the end.

Stan and I played footy on Maxie Fields, whilst dreaming of the future. Footballing days ended as we strolled off a bumpy field in Suffolk in 2003, mere faces in a crowd. Surviving unscathed, I returned to running in April with renewed vigour to become faster and fitter. I had had fun, but I was now ready to go   run.

Faster

Mile 14

'Speed and pace is a temporary place.'

Mark Lankester

In one slight step and a skip, babies were born to run, unbridled, and into the light. Everyone discovers sport, though a few we never try. I for one have never surfed, scuba-dived or ridden a horse. Howbeit, most mortals break into a trot at varying speeds, and by training, we can improve.

Children are endlessly in perpetual motion. For when I saw my niece scamper across the lawn to chase the family cat, I thought yeah girl you have mastered the art. If a drone flew above an infant school playing field, the view might resemble a scene of scattering hyperactive ants. Fast-forward 20 years, those same people appear frozen as if statues.

Trees I climbed as a kid and ran to the shops. Yet if I did so today, critics may cite eccentricity. The modern world we live, full of restraint, workers sit desk bound and drive for hours arriving home exhausted, starved of exercise. In not so distant ages, our forebears performed more physically active tasks to earn a living.

Will Power I call a friend, not the motorsports driver though I am sure he is a nice bloke, but determination and make time to keep fitness. Royal Mail pays Mr Postman to walk, I am lucky in that regard. Albeit, I am inspired by those who strive harder than I, for no other reason than to test the human spirit.

George Mallory the intrepid explorer climbed Everest. For it is there, the mountaineer declared and died trying. No, I have never felt the impulse to risk death. Dangerous pursuits are out, but I embrace pushing the body, so I run.

Humans have two types of muscle fibres in the legs, slow-twitch and fast. Most have an equal ratio. Sprinters may have a higher share of the speedy ones. Improvement in longevity and speed is attainable with whatever nature blessed gene wise.

The sport looks more corporate than ever, with an array of gear to choose. If injuries persist, seek expert advice. Comfort and injury prevention is vital. Roger Bannister ran in shoes akin to the plimsolls I wore in PE at school.

The Oxford flyer broke the four-minute mile. Sure, nature endowed the record breaker with a high proportion of fast switch fibres, but training outstrips attire.

Imagine the body as a car. A decent engine is the ticket to success, but a flat tyre equals disaster. So take care of the feet, a complex mix of tiny bones, ligaments, joints and tendons. A light framed motor vehicle has the potential for speed, but requires a solid base or else falls apart. Runners need strength, so dieting is not the answer, but a healthy diet is.

Writing a book is comparable to marathon training. The words flowed when I first wrote. A few months later, the plot became harder, and progress slower. Close to giving up, inspiration put the pen on track. Imagination of the mind whilst restless is a spellbound journey tougher and more exhausting than any I have undertaken. Yet, I enjoy the struggle.

The 26.2 sign posts a bridge too far, but when breaking distance up into smaller segments, the task becomes achievable akin to drafting a story. Possibilities endless, running clears the head on the streets I love. The tranquillity I sense afterwards makes every step worthwhile, and though not a wonder drug, endorphins are worth bottling.

In the past, I jogged three times a week, but now the routine rolled daily. The pounds fell off as I ran at least a mile that often became five. Weight loss I did not notice, but others did, and pace increased. Lighter, yet stronger, I never cut food intake. People made the usual comments as regards to my physique, but speed was a serious business and not a pie-eating contest.

Remember Jimmy, he said breaking a seven-minute mile was folly, as I struggled to stay the distance on joint outings. Wrong he was, because in time I managed that pace for 12 miles. Life was great when running personal bests in my mid-thirties.

Training with Jim, I slowed so the old timer could keep up, but disguised it as I enjoyed his company.

Months later, at a race, he agreed to wait in the bar afterwards. Instead, I had a pint ready and waiting for him when finished.

While we drank a brew, we laughed recalling the mix-up in the Wimpy years ago. Yes, he once loved the Bay City Rollers, and now forty odd he raved over the Kaiser Chiefs. He always had his finger on the pulse. Yet drifting on dragging up the past, we were a million miles from Maxie Fields and God Save the Queen.

Fit for a lifetime his heart rate was probably lower than mine. Truth be told, we were two lost souls swimming in a fishbowl, running the streets with the same fears. Indian summer it was, for I knew peak fitness was only a brief chapter in the book of life and savoured the taste.

Self-improvement I noticed in its entirety in 2004 at a seven-mile race at Stowmarket. The event appealed because I wanted to hold 6:45 pace for an extended period. Used to the same faces of similar ability huffing and puffing in earshot, this time I was running with the unknown. A few miles in, I spotted Duncan, a faster fellow club runner ahead, as I closed the gap.

Lungs burning, breathing heavy, I searched for the mile markers before our techno saviour Garmin. Halfway round, I checked the wristwatch, confirming splendid news. Pain ignored, I did not wilt. Big Dunc crossed the line within touching distance. He had suffered flu the preceding week. Yet, I was proud to finish in 47:33 the best I could be.

The course had given heart belief, and improvement continued. Internet an unused tool, I waited with bated breath for the results to arrive by post. The top 30 men were often in the paper. An incentive I had in local events. The Bildeston 10k I entered with a chest infection and came in 23rd, but to push my body full of medication was foolish.

Easter Sunday, I was back in Stowmarket for a 10-miler along with 166 runners and one Elvis. With a little less conversation, I strived to break 70 minutes. Yes, I finished a few seconds outside, but never hid. Pain was information. The King sang of a mountain the Lord gave him to climb, but on those Suffolk roads, my only interest was flat road speed.

In May, I arrived in Woodbridge for a 10k to dip under the 40-minute barrier. The week had been awful after a family bereavement. Below par, I had been drinking alcohol and lacked sleep. That day anger in heart I prayed for divine inspiration. This a mission I finished in 41:57 and never pushed harder.

In a sombre place, I learnt I could plough through adversity. The Jaffa 5 two weeks later, I give it ago and ended up 31st, with no mention in the newspaper. No matter, the next morning I awoke to witness the sunrise.

By 2005, I had been running eight years and understood nutrition and training. Speed work I embraced and found a local football pitch, a suitable substitute for a 400-metre athletic track, and ran wide to replicate the distance.

Parks are free, I never took to tennis, and unable to concentrate I worried the caretaker could arrive at any moment to demand cash. Sad to see empty courts locked up from the public. No wonder so few brits have won Wimbledon.

Grass creates a demanding surface when wet. I ran between each goal, and for shorter drills used half the field. This led to a minor accident once. The nets were up between the posts and I rushed straight into one, entwined and tangled. Breaking free, I detected a bloke in the distance, and shot off before he got close.

Armed with a stopwatch, unsophisticated training worked. Ten sprints between the centre spot and goal with 30 seconds recovery. Five laps of the pitch with a minute between each lap. Variations included running hard between two-lamp posts and then slow between the next pair. I did regular press ups but never lifted weights. In later life, I learnt the names of those drills. The long Sunday jog the key to victory, burns fat and boosts endurance.

A Tempo run is a fast-paced work out at the same effort for half an hour to 40 minutes. Fartlek means 'speed play' perfected by a Swedish coach. The technique is to mix a slow and swift pace during the same session. Training faster than normal helps the individual adjust, and slower intervals, enables one to push harder when recovered.

If I trained properly, multiplying my best 10-mile by three gave a rough marathon finish of 3:30. Once, I heard a TV presenter say it was a mark of a decent runner. This the Golden Goose, and within my capabilities. Somewhat matured since and humble, everyman has a goal. Fast running out of time, London 2006 might be my last chance before age confined quality times to a dusty old folder.

During the summer of 2005, local club Jaffa started a junior group and asked if I could help. The sessions flourished, and my son joined. A gofer, I kept the kids occupied using drills I practised in my training, with minor alterations. No, I did not get in London that year, but it was only a matter of time before I dipped under 40 minutes for 10k.

In October, eight years since my first race at Felixstowe, I stood again on the start line for the half marathon confident I could smash 1 hour 30. Faster I felt invincible, but I do wish I knew then what I know today. A 50-year-old man inside a younger body would be a formidable force to behold.

The event morphed into an annual family gathering, and the kids cannot recall a time when I did not run. Dressed in Jaffa red and blue I was at my best in 2005. I was an athlete, or at least sought to be one.

The two-lap race started near the pier and I tried to tackle the first half as a 10k, confident I had enough left for the second. This was confidence, not endorsed by coaches. If I could finish in 42 minutes, I only had to complete the next in less than 48 to break 1.30.

Family support gave a shot of adrenaline, as I arrived at the promenade ready to run round again. That morning, the electronic timer read 44:10, and I now had to motor to achieve my target on a windy seafront.

In a readjusted ambition, I again reached the beach huts with hope. Yet by mile 9, the bear had jumped on my back, and the final four were the hardest ever. Lungs fit to burst and rasping for breath, seagulls shrieked over distance voices.

With the crowd roar close, I figured that if I went flat out, I might grab a PB, but I run out of gas and failed the test. When slumped against a wall, a woman inquired if I was okay. Within a moment, I composed the mind. Agony raged, approaching the leisure centre, as swarms of perceptive athletes overtook as aching legs pulsated and shook.

When I arrived on the promenade, pedestrians were strolling along the course, oblivious there was a race. On the final straight, I resisted the urge to swear at a bloke eating chips I swerved to avoid. Family cheered, and I sprinted to the line. PB achieved, I was never so glad to finish.

Ray Crawford, the Ipswich Town legend, often visited Felixstowe when injured and stepped in the water waste high. The salt helped injuries, and today running coach's advocate ice baths. Afterwards, I waded into the ocean to sooth the bod and fell in, to the amusement of all and sundry. The October North Sea took the breath but revitalised the soul in an instant!

Desperate to run London 2006, I felt I had a realistic chance of breaking 3:30. As expected, a rejection magazine arrived. Never did I contemplate another. Around this time, George Best died. Heartbroken when hearing the news of Bestie, ballot entry failure melted into mere disappointment.

I had no hope, but Bob ran for charity, and then to my surprise, I gained a club place through Ipswich Jaffa without the pressure of raising thousands. Not wasting the opportunity, I hoped for a memory to last for perpetuity. Dad, what that word means, my daughter once said, as she looked up with a twinkle in her eye. 'Forever' I replied with a broad smile, for dreams and legends never fade. Cue Rocky theme, London   here   we   come!

Best Shot

Mile 15

'Believe you can and you're halfway there.'

Theodore Roosevelt

Training for the Flora London Marathon 2006 started in a nine-mile stagger on Boxing Day. Shaky at first, the head cleared. For poisoned by festive cheer and relieved to hit the fresh air, there was a wealth of calories to burn. That year I started to keep a running log, and have continued to do so.

The Wednesday after Christmas, I knocked out 10 of the best in a snowdrift that sucked on the lower limbs as if quicksand. Although pleased with the time, stumbling along Rushmere golf course, the right thigh muscle tightened in a spasm to send a shock wave of pain. The white blanket glistened, as if a fluffy duvet enveloped the fairway, only distinguishable by random flag pins that resembled candles on an ice topped birthday cake.

The blizzard worsened on Friday, and I finished the last third with Uncle Jim. Treadmills akin to marmite, people either embrace or loathe, but indoor jogging has advantages. The weather and traffic is never an issue and saves on the washing of filthy clothes. The conveyer belt of speed furthermore avoids dodging folk whilst on pavements and hopping over curbs.

I trained alone for four months. The solitude I enjoyed and working as a postman gave ample excuse to step out in the afternoons. Howbeit, I helped with the junior group on Monday evenings. Although without a listening device to form a theme tune to my stride, and GPS to record journey travelled, I had space to dream on those Suffolk streets.

Sweet dreams of legends past filled the mind. The visions of the terraces lifted the spirits when the body wilted. Drive rose as if a better man were striving forward. The two Kevin's, Beattie and Keegan shone, and I thought of the Superstar Brian Jacks and James Hunt who drove a fast car, for no run is a bridge too far.

Running changed my life, but football will forever be a passion. For, in no other game do souls on pitch and terrace share so much joy. Howbeit the thrill of being the finest you can be, by dragging one's body forwards on the wet pavements one-step at a time to lift the spirit is a unique gift.

Early on, I felt a dull ache in the front lower leg. The discomfort was as if the bones were bruised and I feared a stress fracture. Yet suffering from doctor phobia, I instead sought a fresh pair of shoes. The comfy style of Nike I prefer. The swoosh logo designed to illustrate the arch of sound and movement.

Shin splints are an irritating injury common in marathoners. Constant pounding on hard surfaces or shabby footwear contributes. The issue didn't persist when switching to the soft country trails. Once finished, I strapped a frozen bag of peas to the leg to relieve inflammation. Pills avoided, I rubbed Ibuprofen gel into the skin and once in sheer desperation sprayed WD40. The placebo effect may have been a blessing.

Therefore, training was a project of self-injurious behaviour. Rest days were two to five miles slow, and I added a mile a week to the long Sunday jaunt. The iconic distance was born from a fable of Pheidippides who raced to Athens to report of triumph at the Battle of Marathon. The goddess Nike personified victory in ancient Greek civilisation. He may have uttered the word with joy before dying of exhaustion.

Nature cruel and unpredictable, running races is a choice, and not life and death, because one can stop. For during a 15 miler, I mulled over a news report I had seen on television. A whale had gotten lost in the River Thames. The Goliath of the Ocean should have been nowhere near the capital. Hurt in a fight for survival in the shallow estuary, the female bottlenose perished despite the valiant efforts of the rescue services.

In January, I travelled to Chelmsford, to take a coaching course. The classroom sparked flashbacks of school, and windowless walls tightened the soul. I half expected Spitfire to smash a wooden ruler across my knuckles, amongst squeaking desks and coughs.

Yet outside on the track, the tension abated and the varied accents that echoed amongst the open space in a picturesque English scene intrigued. The dialects within England's green and pleasant land change in a scant distance travelled. A lad from Southend asked if I had driven there on a tractor, and I returned the serve by mentioning Dylan's bottled tan.

Once back at Ipswich Jaffa, eager to try the drills learnt there were coaches more experienced. Gunga Din more suited to fetching and carrying joined in the sprints to show the kids I could walk the talk. Sixth sense ignored and wearing casual shoes not expecting to run, disaster struck, as a pain shot through the knee.

Bravado I had engaged in before in a football match at my son's birthday party. Frank's dad did likewise on Maxie Fields, performing skills as if circus acts, to the taunts of Stan. Three decades thereafter, morphing into Ralph, I stole the ball at every moment and scored two within minutes. The hat trick on, I blasted another that ricochet smashing plates of jelly and ice cream before retreating to the side-line with intense embarrassment.

Heck, I worked six days a week. The Beatles managed eight, but on a Long and Winding Road, Sunday was the one opportunity for the big run. Forever tired, the urge to sleep in was huge. For I awoke early, still yawning, and knew the challenge and struggle that were dawning.

Wednesday the 6th of March I ran a 17 miler, I know that from my journal. The evening before, I dropped off drinks on route before the wintry, windy night left a pool of tears and a slug nestled on the first bottle's lid. The plan was to hang on for the duration, and ignore pain, rain and brain.

Though tough, I broke the distance up into segments. At 10k, I had a sluggish slime covered drink waiting in Martlesham. On arrival at mile nine, I decided not to return the same way and cut through the woods, thus missing the next water station. The direction I chose harder and cross-country. Fate intervened as a bike approached from a side trail, with a man ringing a bell and screaming abuse.

Stan was recognisable, swaying back and forth peddling home from work, despite sporting a helmet. The machine lightweight, I marvelled at how the frame supported the rider who was now so much wider. The old mate slowed to chat. He carried H2O, or so I guessed. Flat coke, a funky alternative, I took a swig with gusto.

Lance Armstrong, the US cyclist, was his hero having beaten cancer to win so many races. Inspired, Stanley wanted to lose a few pounds, and we talked sport for a few miles. In childhood memories, I forever picture the lad on two wheels and I asked what his fascination was. The philosophy was pure and as simplistic as 30 years earlier. Keep fit, no traffic jams and cheaper than a motor.

Before heading homewards, Stan wished the best for London and I bid him good luck with the Tour de France. For the joker laughed and threw in a funnier one-liner suggesting I sue Mr Barber, for he had not forgotten that I had once used cycle oil on my hair.

A long way from home, for the next half an hour I thought of the American icon. Pain was information to the brain and nothing to fear. See, back in 2006, I was unaware of the future drug scandal. Bradley Wiggins mentioned that the guy was inspirational and it's not a controversial statement, but a fact. Fools air brush memories, and for the record, a pal lost a team quiz when suggesting Lance had landed on the Moon.

Seventeen miles in 2:16 and watch stopped with satisfaction I had flown 'clean'. Yet I soon reached for the first aid cabinet. The edge yeah, I often wonder if I could have resisted the temptation to take performance-enhancing drugs. The man I cannot judge until wearing those proverbial shoes and facing such adversity.

In February I finished a half marathon with a virus, then crashed and burned trying to stick to a 7.45 pace, faster than I expected at London. Not wanting pressure, I entered no build up events and an 18-mile run quicker than expected yielded further faith. Man chooses arbitrary figures to tackle. On the continent, people consider 30k a fair trot.

Goals scored to sounds of cheers on green fields with a ball at feet can fill a skilful soul full of pride. Yet roars of traffic and a look of nothingness when pedestrians pass, magnifies the loneliness of a distance runner. None of them received a hero's welcome. Until that is the big day itself, when for a few hours millions dream of sharing your journey.

The penultimate biggie arrived, the hard castle of 19, with few dress rehearsals left. That morn water tumbled from the heavens. Yet regardless, I wore a vest with faith in the deluge relenting, heading out on Bucklesham Road, and avoiding the muddy trails. The rainfall diminished, but not a gale that struck from the front and sides, but never from the rear to propel the aching torso forward.

Soaked to the skin, damp clothes are useless in freezing conditions. With wet feet and numb toes, once I crossed the bridge over the A14 the sun rose as if by magic. In a brief span of woodland, I took off my vest to ring out and dried the face, having ridden the onslaught. The final five miles were pleasant, and I felt contentment as I moderated the speed well on target.

Three weeks before London, the crucial period of training had arrived, the last big run. Experts suggest a fortnight, but I knew my body. Runners have stormed a great 20- miler approaching marathon date and paid the price still suffering fatigue. If I developed a problem, I could sort out any niggles.

Felixstowe, a straight route, I fretted over heading out so far. Pound in pocket I could phone a friend if the twisted knee troubled. Pouring outside, I counted on the rain to lift as I sipped a mug of tea. The gear I choose was the race day wear of black Nike vest and shorts. For I am forever impressed with the striking pose of the New Zealand athletes. Of whom John Walker was one and the first to run a mile in under 3:50.

The faithful Casio Watch started from zero after touching my toes twice in the briefest of warm-ups. The start was uphill and over a bridge towards the local church. Often on training runs, I drove there cutting out the incline, as the stride out whilst sorting a rhythm of echoed huffs is laboured.

Once past Saint Augustine's, the road flattened, and the tears from the sky continued. British weather a pain. A runner can experience, wind, sun, sleet in a single morning. For in England's blue suburban skies, if the heavens are not pouring, just wait a while. There is a price to pay for those lush green pastures of home.

Mile 2, I neared the Suffolk Showground, the scene of an agricultural show held once a year. The rain stung the eyes as hair gel dripped from the brow, running along the Old Levington Road. The melody of birds and the faint rubble of distance traffic formed a classic sweet symphony.

Open fields lay both sides of the country lane and welcomed the full brunt of the elements. For a second, I considered adjusting the journey to stay closer to home. Giving one's self a good lecture, I stormed eastward.

Comfort rose within, knowing I was to be joining in a common goal with 30,000 other entrants bolstered by spectators from start to finish. Lonely bitter winter mornings are when the marathoner finds out if the guts and want are there. Marathon day is the last step of a multitude of hard runs.

The shower subsided, and the milestones passed as I drifted in cruise control through Trimley and then Walton. On the hour mark, eight miles was registered a tad too swift with a long road ahead. Therefore, I breathed in deep to calm body and mind. For every minute gained early on, are two lost in the long run.

To this day, I still enjoy a sense of accomplishment arriving in Felixstowe. Daft, because I often stride out further. When the North Sea became near, the wind and spray of life's joy whistled through the hair on one's head. The sun sparkled, overdubbed with the shriek of seagulls and the sight of the Fish Bar Regal.

Arms red, getting a tan in the freezing rain, I sensed a loss with no one there to share the promenade of solitary fame. Yet I saw a vision in my mind of my son and daughter, buckets and spades in hands framed in front of the deep blue water.

Halfway now, I ran to the water's edge, as the legs buckled on the beach whilst glancing at the dock that was once the gateway of Viking raiders and many invaders that shaped the place I call home. The 200-metre stagger was arduous as the pebbles jumped up to bite the ankles. Yet when I breathed deep and splashed the body with seawater, the endorphins flowed from head to toe, plugging the soul into the mains of life's electricity.

Do it again, was the state of play, as I turned back west, blinded with a wave of sunshine in a soaking wet vest. An elderly couple stared as I bid the folks good morning. The croaky voice with salt spray on the tongue suggested dehydration. The old guy wore a black tee shirt with the words Abbey Road. For the youth of the sixties were now approaching 64.

Lucozade found at the half marathon point and sugar levels restored, the watch read 1:37 and the shaky frame of man ploughed forward, with no time to wait.

Close to home, a Dylan tune resonated in my head and the lyrics that flowed were a perfect finale. A rolling stone alone journeying homeward, clothes dirty but hands clean, the finish was the most welcoming sight I had ever seen.

Twenty finished in 2 hours 34 minutes can be as hard as London on tired legs. Understand during training, I had run 40 per week and 46 when on holiday. Although not high mileage, back then, I was oblivious of other people's regimes. Social media I was yet to discover.

A neighbour mentioned seeing me jogging whilst filling the car at Sainsbury's a mile from home. However, I never bothered to tell a humble boast of distance covered. There were no cameras, spectators, or medals, but I had earnt the tools to break barriers on the highways where faith carries weary souls.

For I wanted to fly high and feeling the pain in the morning rain, I hoped to live forever. The mist of my breath blew into the wind as I experienced a world I could never see locked in a car or watching TV. In a line of fantasy and reality, a crusade is a saviour, and a learning curve in a horizon of dreams.

The long run gave one enormous confidence. At London, fuelled with a week's rest, I could blitz 3 hours 30. Experts consider '20', halfway. Ten thousand metres is a tough distance after running that far. This is the point many runners hit the 'wall' and engines stool. A term used to describe what happens when stored energy in muscles runs out, often between 16 to 22 miles.

I hoped for the crowd to carry me onward when my body became tired and my fuel supply had long since expired. When I was a kid, I went to Sunday school. I remember a story of a man who climbed a mountain. God told insisted he was there by his side, despite only one set of footprints. For the lord had carried him. I am not a churchgoer, nor a nonbeliever, but a guiding light back then drove me to surpass my own ability.

The television series 'Run for Glory' I viewed with intrigue as Sally Gunnell and Steve Cram trained a group of novices to finish the London Marathon. Heart-warming and inspirational, one lad Clint suffered a life-threating health condition. He had a point to prove and pushed the body to the limit the day we met on the streets of the capital.

The taper is when runners have peaked trimming training to recover and build up strength. It is a palpable quandary, pull back too early and lose the edge, or too near and risk injury or fatigue. So, I tailed off for three weeks. The rest bite played tricks, but after the 20- miler, I caught a bug, so it was easy to relax with a waspish chest.

I abstained from training the week leading up to London and turned 38 a few days before, full of doubt. The Sunday before, I drove the equivalent distance to Aldeburgh beach with family. The knee hurt pressing the clutch pedal, so what chance was there on marathon day smashing the feet on concrete?

Lost in thought, sitting on the seafront, was my lowest ebb as I watched the kids play in-between gazing out at the ocean. Twenty miles separate England from France at the closest spot. Ten kilometres further than that was a terrifying doom laden prospect. Imagine, sat with arms round knees, I must have cut a solitary figure. The family glanced over and waved, and I nodded back with a frown and not much vigour.

Aldeburgh is a quaint Suffolk town near Thorpeness, home to a boating lake. Visitors will strive to find a view more English amongst tea cafes, antique shops and charming countryside. Mum and Dad had a caravan, a quick stroll from the beach where a sculpture called the 'Scallop' rises from the pebbles.

The giant shell varies at differing angles resembling a bird viewed between the towns. Whilst running through the village, the form morphed into two men rowing a boat. If visiting, check out the art from various vantage points and the House in the sky, not forgetting a shop that does an excellent apple pie.

Well prepared, logic prevailed in blocking those negative thoughts as the event approached. Wednesday I headed to the Big Smoke on the train, to pick up my race number. On the underground, I noticed an array of running shoes on shuffling feet and followed their lead to the expo.

For we only live 70 miles from Greenwich and did not stay over the weekend, but travelled on the Sunday with Ipswich JAFFA, whose full name may confuse the most competent local rapper. That said I must digress. Ed Sheeran emerged from Suffolk where a castle stands on a hill, and whilst I ran those country trails, he was honing his craft with a poetic wit   and   melody.

London Marathon II

'The essence of being human is that one does not seek perfection.'

George Orwell

The first London Marathon was a thrill, but for the sequel, I sought to break 3 hours 30. St George's Day April 23rd 2006 was a fitting occasion to take on the well-trodden streets of Londinium.

George the Turkish born Roman soldier became the paragon of virtue in England centuries after marching through Old Blighty. England's capital has been the epicentre of a vibrant tapestry of immigration for two millennia. Or what of Shakespeare, for William departed this Earth on that date, and gave our land a unique prose.

Wise men and clowns race not knowing the speed of fate. The phrase 'Citius, fortius, functum' means 'faster, stronger and fitter' in Latin and if one confesses to lacking talent, and success has been through willpower alone, the testimony is a mere smokescreen. For failure expected has no case to plead. Be thankful man's limitations are without limits.

Restless the night before, I dreamed I stood on the start line with feet of clay. Work boots on, I stared ahead on a road that sank into a murky fog to the echo of ships' horns and the chime of Big Ben. The nightmare worsened when Gordon the scot of Ramsey appeared to yell abuse for neglecting one's trainers.

Cheese makes me dream, and I had eaten a wealth of cheesy pizza. Despite limited zeds, I was bang up for the struggle, howbeit not a dragon slayer, but a minor player amid thousands of marathoning pilgrims.

Ipswich JAFFA organised a bus for folk who included my wife, children, parents, in-laws and nephew. Once there, I recognised a chap from the local gym. The younger man I envied. Rob often furloughed from training to party for months and then returned to discard surplus weight as if a boxer. Never have I had that inner faith.

Adrenaline in overdrive, I talked continuously and feared burning up the restless energy required when completing 26.2 miles. If I achieved the target and then never run again, that was okay. Running to finish is tough, but to drive the frame for a time can be a risky game of Russian roulette ending in a Suffolk Punch.

The radio played amongst the rustle of food, small talk and the odd announcement from driver Pete. Gnarls Barkley's smash hit 'Crazy' formed the theme tune to the day's events. Gallant exploits on the roads of the Great Wen looked fun in 1981. For 25 years later the body knew, pumping juice to the heart that beated as if a drum, expecting the big run.

Live strong, for existence is too short to be fraught with anxiety. Fear and forty were bedfellows, and I wanted life's pause button. Ordinary I was, envying the famed achievers and unsure of the course of destiny, the lust for life burnt a flaming path.

The bus dropped off at Blackheath, and family and friends waved us off with best wishes as we disembarked with sports bags on shoulders. Rob and mate Mark stayed close, thirsty for guidance when learning I had run London. The lads were targeting sub 3:30 and appeared a comparable pace. Yet Mark's face mirrored my angst.

Fear dampens the fire of the strongest and brave. If harnessing those demons and controlling flames, man can achieve more than expected, and never become infected by self-doubt. Yep, I had seen too many Rocky films. Howbeit as I joked whilst making light of the Urban Everest, the fella rose and focused.

Thousands wandered around with white plastic bags adorned with race numbers as we hunted for a spot on the field to get sorted. A crisp morning with the prevailing shower, the conditions were ideal. Gear on under tracksuit bracing to run; I fixed the number 25032 to chest with six safety pins, so as not to lose on passage.

Head to toe in Nike, I resembled a poster boy for the American company, albeit in an awkward stance. Champion chip tied to lace, the device registered splits on route. Right-footed, dominant leg chosen, fingers attaching the tag were cumbersome as passer-by leant a hand. The lady might well have been famous. Those types of incidents happen on race day, as if stepping into the television.

The scene was familiar as I had trod the same space in 1999, but tried my best to absorb the surroundings, knowing I may never return. Hot air balloons rested in the distance. One was a green dragon and I was unsure whether they were for show or were to float high into the city sky.

The elite runners and wheelchair athletes included Felix Limo, Deena Kastor, David Weir and Shelly Woods. Olympic rowers Matthew Pinsent, Steve Redgrave, James Cracknell were there as well as swimmer Karen Pickering from my hometown Ipswich. On a sad note, Britain's finest Paula Radcliffe was missing through injury.

Jade Goody, presenter Adrian Childs, and Chef Gordon Ramsey, were familiar TV celebrities who had entered, and I spotted Bob Hope. No, he was not the legendary Hollywood actor but Tony Audenshaw from the ITV soap opera Emmerdale.

The biggest charity earner on the planet in one day raises millions. You can see the suffering and joy on every competitor. That year I chose to run for E.A.C.H a local hospice that cares for youngsters with a life threating illness. For the event is the runner's version of Live Aid and gets bigger annually.

Bags secured on the orange trucks, we headed to the mass start. The murmur of a helicopter above formed a motion picture soundtrack. Mark and Rob started in the third corral, a sane position for those aiming for three and a half hours of foot pounding. Although I feared the stampede in pen one, I zipped off there, much to the lad's hilarity. The zone was a quarter full and the elite athletes were several metres ahead.

Sebastian Coe, wearing a blue fleece stood a stone's throw away on the rostrum, was ready to press the horn. As I glanced behind, the second enclosure burst at the seams. Runners strutted around as if peacock in a coup and I skipped back a tad inferior. When I asked an athletic fellow what time desired, Geordie dulcet tones muttered 2:45. So, I retreated further, despite sporting the brand of victory.

Minutes before the race, I mimicked the flyer's warm-up act. Though feeling a fraud, the front line guaranteed an excellent getaway from the outset. Despite expecting officials to yank me outta there, I had slimmed and did not look out of place. Seb pressed the horn, the elites sprinted off, and we followed within 30 seconds. Go for it...

Amazingly 33,578 hearts and minds were charging towards The Mall joined in a common goal. Every man and woman had their own story on a pathway to glory, whether a world record, memories of a loved one, the triumph in defeating illness, or a personal test.

Phew, running along Shooters Hill Road, I knew I was moving too quick. Red double lines on the side of the road instead of yellow, I had a blue line to find painted along the entire optimum route. In theory, if followed, one should not have to cover more than marathon distance because weaving left to right forces marathoners to run further. Dashes in road as if in Morse code, presumably saved paint.

Runners from Greenwich and St Johns joined on the cusp of the three-mile balloon arch, not as overcrowded as expected. Flora advertisement hoarding, balloons, and barriers of green and yellow blended exquisitely with the bushes and trees whilst umbrellaed spectators smiled and cheered.

Except for a bloke in an orange clown wig, I saw no one in fancy dress. Early approaching the next marker, I settled and picked up bottled water. People overtook, and likewise I passed a few, as adrenaline surged.

The target I set one's self required a pace of eight-minute miles. Beat the clock, boom-boom the sparks flew, as a tune locked into the brain in a way I cannot explain. For the lyrics, I know not. Keep on moving for success is earnt, 7:35, 7:40, and 7:34. Boom, 23 miles to go!

Perfect start achieved, I arrived at the fourth mile arch in a sound position. The road downhill, I checked out the Thames amongst a plethora of support. As I headed along Woolwich Church Street, I recognised Clint from the BBC television series 'Run for Glory' running by my side.

He must have stormed the early miles. Steve Cram throughout the programme chastised him for setting out too fast. We spoke for a brief time. As I mentioned before, he lived with a life threatening condition and sadly, a few years later died. Privileged to have met him, I hope he was proud with what he achieved.

The marathon changes people's lives. Anyone who is a runner, or wishes to be a marathoner, should run Londinium at least once. London Pride beer advertisements featured prominently nearing the Cutty Sark, while the harmony of steel drums pumped endorphins through veins.

The Clipper on display in Greenwich since 1954 struck a striking pose. So making hay while the sun refused to shine, I clocked 47:58 for 10k. The vessel was the speediest of its day and ruled the waves in the 1800s. For England was always a sea-faring nation, and with that thought I experienced a pang of sadness seeing the ship landlocked.

Deptford quieter, with fewer spectators, I fretted over the throbbing knee that held out in training. Two minutes within schedule, for a few seconds I stretched behind a bus shelter. Mile eight from my personal standpoint is on the cusp of a distance run and a transition to conquer. Yet entering the Docklands, rhythm of body and mind relaxed into zoneful motion.

Another tip I had taken from the earlier marathon, was that an abundance of drink stations existed and the crowd supplied plenty of food, which was the reason I ran light. Sweets and chocolate handed out by smilers I ate half a lion bar at one point.

Ten miles in with the body in long-run territory, for the first time I felt the elements, as the wind and rain whipping across the river Thames slapped the face. Ambulances lined the streets, as if a cloak of safety, blending a camouflaged yellow and green to the backdrop of an epic sporting scene.

A familiar face caught up around the 11-mile mark. Another member of the gym whom I had not realised was running. His target was 2:59, so I expected the conversation to be brief. Gary mentioned the fact I never used locker 13 in the changing rooms, even when no alternative was available. No, I am not superstitious, but I see scant reason to tempt fate.

On Jamaica Road, the support became louder, and Gazza pushed on as I bid him good luck. Yet his marathon did not go to plan, as he battled injury in the last eight. Success and failure can be a spin of a coin.

Tower Bridge approaching halfway is the best part of the day apart from the finish. Brave working men completed the Victorian marvel in 1894. Guy Ritchie's movie 'Sherlock Holmes' is worth a peek, just to spot the capital in the late 1880s, and the partially built landmark in CGI. The last erected over the Thames River until the Millennium Footbridge.

The half marathon mark registered 1:43:15. Not long after, I received a tremendous boost when hearing Dad's voice boom over the throng. So I turned back and saw my daughters little face in crowded confusion and I touched her hand, saying hi to family. Get going, they shouted as not wanting me to squander time.

Seconds lost were nothing to the mental lift provided. Benumbed in April rain spectators smiled despite the weather. For it is just another run without the sea of humanity and the noise and sound of celebration. An empty house is four walls, but the soul is the people inhabiting the space.

The marathon unique, I only think in imperial measurements. If I look at someone, I guess their height in feet and inches, not in metric. Many years ago, no exact length existed, and races varied between 22 to 25 miles. The 42.195 kilometres first used in the London Olympic Games in 1908, the distance, we know to this day. The Prince of Wales thought it an excellent idea to have the start and finish at Windsor Castle so his children could appreciate the spectacle.

The 1924 Olympics in Paris, France is where they set the distance as standard. So next time you struggle in the final straight, blame the Royal family for the extra 385 yards. Okay, joking aside, it adds to the charm, which makes it so special.

At the mile 14, I ran towards athletes fleeter of foot. Gebrselassie and Hendrick Ramaala sporting a red bandanna were zipping along on route to the Embankment. The next few miles were vital as I had to concentrate and feared losing time.

West Ferry Road heading into the Docklands I ploughed on through, out of the comfort zone. If I hit the wall so be it, I came here to thrive not survive. An arrogant comment when written on the page, I had to big myself up with words of fire to fuel the stride.

The crowd sparse in Canary Wharf, the tall buildings blocked the light, and I thought it a window cleaner's utopia. Decem milia passuum, St George might have said as the watch read 2:39, with no time to waste.

Twenty miles in the pace slipped, as I heard a mobile phone call out in dulcet Americano tones. The perpetrator held a 3:30 banner whilst pacing eight other runners, who overtook one after another as if a duck with her babes. For dressed in black I felt an ugly duckling and legs were buckling.

Ten kilometres a fair run on battered bones, exhausted and inspired tears poured from weary eyes as tension released as if working the gears searching the soul for coal.

Breath deep, the sound was as if a steam train pulling from the platform as lungs drew oxygen to propel the human frame. Do not think. The brain burns calories. Move, lengthen the stride, when nowhere to hide. Determination and pain is 5k from Her Majesties Palace.

On the highway to heaven, I could see the Tower of London. Near enough to the end to burn what embers remained, I hauled back time, and kept within target. At the 23 marker, I heard my family cheer and held arms aloft, ploughing forward with no cobbled streets to bend ankles.

Fuel tank low, I weaved bodies as if dribbling round traffic cones with a ball at feet. With only a few more minutes of pain, the body pushed hard, because the lacking of guile in the face of discomfort lay the foundation of eternal regret.

Blackfriars Underpass I passed through sharpish, evoking scenes of individual struggle back in 1999. Now in a positive mind-set, I recalled the tunnel as being downhill. Soon a guiding light appeared, as I returned into the celebration of life. Confidence high the last mile was to be one long lap of honour.

The atmosphere increased along the Embankment, as if transported into a picture postcard of the capital. With the 'London Eye' in view, the mind can play tricks. Many think they are finished when the iconic sights appear, and bodies shut down in response. Aware there was still hard work ahead, the eyes widened with a grimaced stare.

The blue line now impossible to follow, I dodged runners understanding their pain thankful I had not yet stumbled. Running out of time, I clocked Big Ben and headed past Parliament Square into Birdcage walk.

With a sideways glance at Buck House, I met Boudica, queen of the Iceni, who fought against the Romans, in a stunning show of British resistance. Corner turned with 200 metres to go, and the watch reading three thirty plus one, Union Jack flags fluttered in the wind, either side of The Mall.

The pink road ahead glistened in the drizzle, to form the most exquisite sight I had ever seen. The yellow gantry grew larger and, although hurting, I never felt stronger lifting the arms of pain. Official finish time 3 hours 32 minutes and 13 seconds.

Best shot given I had no regrets. Once composed, I stumbled over to have a photo taken. Shame I did not have a mirror, for I looked a mess with a quiff that had suffered miles of stress. Medal round neck, with goody bag in hand, I found a Mars Bar and Banana. Fruit chosen to avoid chocolate goo, I staggered to find a place to rest weary limbs.

For it shocked me, the condition of many of the finishers who lay by the roadside out of camera shot. The aftermath, the comedown, the tears and relief painted a picture beyond belief. Heads rose from silver blankets as if homeless people sleeping rough.

True, I had given up smoking years earlier, but there were space next to a lad smoking as I sat with a sigh. Lucozade opened with a twist I borrowed a smoke. For having sucked in more oxygen than a barrage balloon, I felt no guilt despite the odd scornful stare.

Family waited at the greeting bays and a pal filmed the reunion in the hugging maze. On watching the film back, I wore a tracksuit now three sizes too large. For the Nike Oregon track top bought when a bigger man will forever remind me of the Goddess of Victory.

Time to kill before the bus left we strolled round Waterstone's bookstore. Good to keep moving we discovered a pub where we shared stories of the day's events, and the strangest tale made perfect sense. The shoes although worn, an invisible force carried one forward when legs stumbled.

On the coach, Rob wore slippers, a clever ploy. Slow to catch up with technology, I expected a club member scrap paper in hand to ask for finish times. Results were now online and the Nokia Brick bleeped with friends enquiring tales of Londidium. The bleep was a sound of annoyance, for I was yet to discover mute, in an era of no bowler hats worn with a suit.

The marathon never changed one's destiny, but inspired one to do so, a subtle distinction. Success does not create happiness, or failure misery. Though life is not black and white, London was technicolour. Roll credits. Not so fast, the toughest challenge was yet to come, the nemesis older. The Silent Assassin stealth of foot was to catch a running man unawares.

Ye Ode Fool

Mile 17

'Beowulf, green fields and river so blue, voices a distant echo and a treasure trove of forgotten prose, our Suffolk twang sprung from Saxon soil.'

Mark Lankester

Post Marathon Londinium, I ran twice in three weeks. There is nothing amiss with taking a break, but in a blink of an eye the Woodbridge 10k was nigh. Despite limited training, in hope of the ace of spades I was self-assured a PB was on the cards.

Chip timing was in practice. Unfamiliar Tec I had only experienced on the streets of the capital. The popular annual spectacle started outside a public school on Burkitt Road. Parked within the 40-acre estate, eager runners collected race numbers. Founded in 1557 as free schooling for the underprivileged of Ipswich, the seat of learning has presided on the site since 1864.

When I picture private schools, I cannot help but visualise a bygone age of flowing black capes and Latin verse. Harry Potter was huge at the time, and when we drove into the grounds, I half expected to see Alnwick Castle. The young wizard was born in a wonky house in Lavenham near Hadleigh. That much is true.

For I am one of the common people more acquainted with the tradesman's entrance. Famous pupils include Luke Roberts who played Ser Arthur Dayne in 'Games of Thrones' and Nick Lowe, the songwriter, and singer who sang of breaking glass.

Cruelty is a kindness, a shakesperianism Nicholas may well of nicked, guitar in hand influenced by a folkish Suffolk melody when penning the hit record 'Cruel to be Kind'. For, with a twist of English rhyme, I love the album 'Jesus of Cool' from the lad that frequented that school.

Eight miles in land from the sea the town thrived on ship construction and sail making of whom Sir Francis Drake were a customer. The Deben rises quick as I once discovered running along the banks on route to Felixstowe. For the zest of fitness had become a mere by-product of embracing nature.

The training run started as I observed boats, mud berthing and the flapping wings of Black-tailed Godwits. Kyson Point is a brief stretch of mudflats where folk can sit and savour the tranquil view. Howbeit, on return, a blonde female muck splattered runner approached to warn the tide was high.

The estuary had claimed the soil. Twenty metres wading through the water, with sodden feet in muddy shoes, was a curious passage to choose. Virtual runs on motorised belts will never eclipse the tidal power, smell, and sound of Suffolk woven in sails floating by Gods county trails.

Poet Edward FitzGerald was a Woodbridge son who once wrote that life flies. In an era of Industrial change and invention, could Ed have imagined the future? For a UFO trail weaves through Rendlesham Forest and on Station Road stands Lilac Thyme's florist.

The Lankester name has survived within or near the riverside for centuries. For the surname uncommon, I dream Dutch settlers sharing the moniker sailed to Old Blighty and settled on the banks of the River Deben.

Okay, back to race day and the Hilly Beast of runners fear. The course reversed in 2002 is still tough, though the slow climb out of town is now a decent, albeit one or three brutal slopes to conquer.

Long ago, the annual gathering took place in July and clashed with the town's church service. To accommodate this, organisers moved the start to 12pm. Since my first race, Woodbridge Shufflers have held the event in May.

Stood poised to run, I waved to the family with Buttrum's Windmill framing the scene. Dutch influence, one surmised, for the region of the East Angles is flat. For Mr Windy Miller valued tradition in the village of Camberwick Green, and Brian Cant Ipswich born and breed narrated the yarn.

Although a sloping riverside parish, the event started downhill, and with the help of gravity, I flew quicker than the tale I expected. The knees took the brunt, and I feared the joints lack of stability as I charged past the Town Hall and a cluster of rustic inns and boutiques. Howbeit not neglecting the Bull Hotel where poet Lord Tennyson once stayed as I strived not to yield.

Head gazing to the sky to steady ones stride the limbs buckled passing under the timber-framed weighbridge that hung from the Ye Olde Bell and Steelyard. The building dates from 1550 and the antique that once weighed farm produce is one of two that survive in England.

Fate and timing are odd bedfellows, and I often wondered if a chariot misguided might strike the bygone apparatus. Today as I write 12 years on a lorry has just slammed into the living history.

There is a narrow corner and bend at the belly of Market Hill. As I clambered the first incline, the legs curved to jelly and the knee that weathered the marathon crumbled. Unable to launch the wilting frame, the wall avoided in London appeared on the sleepy slopes of Suffolk.

Bereft of spirit, I tumbled out and triggering the timing mat on the finish line cutting across the road defeated within less than a mile. Organisers had trouble removing a world record from the results. Though not a complete debacle, the kids entered the fun run.

A few days later, the 'East Anglian Daily Times' published a photograph of me near the front of the field wearing number 316. For today, the swifter lad resembles an intense friend approaching a crossroad in one's life.

On the edge of Woodbridge, a round yellow Pac-Man smiles proudly. Teenagers sprayed a face on the sand bin in the late eighties, Stan's calling card and a reminder of a lost generation. Thirty years ago, fresher faced, we probed for raves in the terrain. Much to the race director's scorn, I flung the plastic timing chip in said place, for I was not to know the tag were reusable.

The emoji grin has faded, one's hair no longer grows faster than weeds, and I abstain from smoking and lounging on top decks of buses. Instead, I should have studied the arts. For I knew nothing of the wordsmiths and artisans who roamed this land, apart from a revolving disc bought spinning the harmony of Shakespears Sister.

History a battered scar on memory I had yet to notice whilst the heart beated young and bold. World Cup and a well-earned summer's rest, Rooney fumed. Ronaldo's Portugal tamed the Three Lions and a flicker of depression flowed at the thought of old age if England were ever champions elect.

Time for a holiday and overnight we flew to the birthplace of the Olympian goddess Aphrodite. Lost in dreams flying through the clouds, I awoke early the next dawn. Without a care, I set out for a jog whilst the family slept.

To run on the curve of silvery sand dipping into blue waters was another world, and within minutes, I was in deserted territory. Despite the tranquil setting, I felt listless. Greek Mythology is rich in legends of Gods rising from the ocean such as the wife of Poseidon. For I did not see Amphitrite dance but a naked elderly mortal.

Startled and in a land of confusion, a Genesis of adrenaline surged as I put in a sprint to avoid embarrassment. Unclad bodies appeared with every stride as old as the rocks as I averted one's gaze through the sunlit morning dusty rays of scratched sun glassed shades.

That afternoon, relaxing poolside, I told the children not to jog with wet feet. Later I bypassed my advice, tiptoed to the bar at the bottom of a concrete stairwell, and tumbled backwards, the head thumping on steps.

The sound was nauseating, echoing a bowling ball striking the floor. The rear of the skull split as if a watermelon as I lay with blood seeping as if a fountain along one's face. Desperate not to faint, I staggered into the open air of women's screams.

A brave rep held the back of my scalp together, awaiting the ambulance. Sown up with 18 stitches, sporting a bandage for the entire stay, I have a visible scar to this day. Stood out as if wearing a clown's wig, I mingled more than usual with yarns to tell of jogging hell.

New cultures and travelling abroad enjoyed, I miss England within a week. For I cherish rain, wind or shine. Yes, we moan of the weather, but once home I could not wait to discover fresh trails in the place that glows green.

Running had taken on a renewed meaning. No longer was I in the grip of fitness and speed, but enchanted by the pure joy of nature. Suffolk shines a historic rustic grace and folk pass a drinking den known as the Unruly Pig on route the land of Saxon Kings. So if you seek such a place, remember the name that is Sutton Hoo.

Back home whilst running again in Blighty, stitching pricked as if pins pressed into scalp. Rendlesham Forest beckoned. For an eternity, I ran through an underpass of trees. Woodland twigs crackled to fire a quiver through one's spine, for the eerie silence was no ally of mine.

Jogging past a village green, I see folk in white stood while people applaud with two men with a bat and another flinging a red ball. Cricket, the gentleman's game, is such a thrill to watch on a fine summer's day. Sometimes I wonder why I quit these shores to travel abroad, because stuck in a 1950s postcard on a Sunday in Suffolk I can never become bored.

The eye of the tiger had gone, and the angel on one's shoulder had flown. True, running benefits mental health and wellbeing, but life is a harmony of balance and the sport grew into a family affair. Every summer local clubs hold a series of Friday evening races. Often I watched instead of slipping on the Nikes, and both my children ran the fun runs at an early age.

The heart a shifting place, as the competitive urge dwindled, the kids inspired and thoughts of another marathon burnt a glimmer of light. Life a cycle a fresh man appeared, wearing different gear as if to shed the rot to keep the best alive.

Sport an analogy, forty loomed an inky foreboding cloud. George Foreman, pugilisms force of nature proved age were no barrier only a doubt-laden carrier. For I lived in hope of eternal youth on a road of contentment that is so hard to find, if not in body but the fretful mind.

Now choosier with races, I trained smart and fixated on the distance I had a chance of a PB. Stamina significant I chipped away at the 13.1 mile, knocking off a few seconds here and there. Great Bentley on an icy winter's day in February 2007, personal best ran two months before the age of 39 the countdown had begun.

River running became the trail of choice and one was the Gipping flowing from Mendlesham Green, through rustic villages to meet the Orwell. For distance is an 18-mile run to Ipswich along the bank from Stowmarket as waters flow.

Zen tranquillity filled the body passing the lock gates that opened the fresh water, breathing in the Suffolk air and hearing the echoes of cowbells and the odd country fare. Plan set, I hoped for a wet weather test wearing a Jaffa vest.

Fate had dealt a hand nearing Ipswich. A poster fixed to a gate advertised a race in the old market of Stow dated three weeks before The Big Four-Oh. One more crack of the whip my friend, before the word 'vet' signals the end.

Easter Sunday 2008, I prepared to run the first Joe Cox Half Marathon, hosted by Stowmarket Striders. That morn, driving to pick up two mates new to running, the weather looked bright, until a flurry of sleet struck the windscreen.

The dulcet tones of Paul Weller and Bono filled the motor to elevate my ever-changing mood. People differ pre-race, a few relax and others such as I burn up nervous energy. On a training run, I can slow if weary, but push to the limit in races for the payoff.

The snow fell, and on arrival, the landscape shone a picture postcard. Stowmarket is 15 miles east of Bury Saint Edmund, where Charles Dickens the famous English writer based the novel Pickwick Papers.

If visiting check out The Angel Inn where thee wordsmith often stayed, not forgetting The White Horse Hotel in Ipswich. As I gazed out of the window, I imagined a wintry Victorian scene that may have inspired him when writing 'A Christmas Carol'.

On my postal route in Barham, hidden within the undergrowth, a few red bricks remain of what was once a workhouse for the poor. Bulldozers demolished the visual reminder of deprivation in 1963. For this place was Mr Dickens' inspiration for Oliver Twist.

Dickensian has become a byword to depict the antiquated. Yet the accounts he wrote of poverty read as if in modern Britain. Writing gives one's thoughts a voice never heard from my lips, unless induced from too many vodka sips.

Whilst bemoaning lack of warm gear, with great expectations, we wondered if the race were to go ahead. In the company of fearless compadres, there was no turning back. Runners slithered to the start point as I slipped on old socks over hands. Relaxed, I looked upon the morning as a workout whilst fling a snowball at a pal. When he ducked, the missile struck a poor girl on the head.

Two years after London, less disciplined, the incident was typical. Alcohol consumed the night before races and eating what I choose speed faltered. Where the streets have no name, the clock ticks slow to dull the pain as if a beguiling steam train rolling on in the quintessentially English rain.

In those days, one could enter events on spec. Online entry was recent, and I entered via the post. Later, we learnt that only 50 percent of the pre-entrants turned up, howbeit 35 hardy souls stumped up cash on the day, and carried on regardless.

The route took runners through the villages of Buxhall, Rattlesden and Brettenham with the odd incline. Concerned with keeping one's feet, not as icy as expected, the soft snow was manageable. Finished in 1:42:11, slower than scheduled, I was glad I got up and went for it. Life is for living, so why waste a morning yawning.

Medals were rare back then, and the memento was a Mars Easter Egg. Cooling in frozen rain, and adrenaline in overdrive, I wolfed an abundance of chocolate and chatted to whoever cared to listen. After chewing the fat, or should I say my chocy treat, I returned to find the lads stood shivering waiting for a lift. Oh dear, they were not best pleased.

Self-belief and confidence are priceless. The mind is a persuasive tool and age became a psychological barrier once 40. In February 2009, I finished the Great Bentley Half a mere second shy of a best time. As I strode to the tape, I am sure negativity made one stumble in the last 200 metres. For in the words of the inimitable Mr D, I forged the chains I wore in life.

Spring turned to summer, and the holiday season arrived. If you mark a straight line westwards from Felixstowe, you will arrive in Borth Beach a quaint seaside town near Aberystwyth in Wales.

When we arrived, I noticed a flyer advertising a Sunday morning10k on the sandy shore. Flat and compact, the course was 5 km to the dunes at Ynyslas, and then back. Trunks of ancient trees from a long-lost forest appear at low tide and I was sure no nudist ventured out on a wet day on the west coast of Britain.

There were 50 runners that included a favourable turn out from Aberystwyth AC. I was top to toe in Ipswich Jaffa colours and a perma-tanned fellow asked my personal best. For I was a stranger and I could tell he sought to check all rivals in a quest for victory.

Chariots of Fire sprang to mind as we scampered across the shore. Today, the film has become nostalgic for the eighties soundtrack as the musicians wrestle with the technology. Somewhat out of tune man and machine, imperfection makes us. As I ran the return leg, I could see the finish throughout as the wind whistled across the sizzling water that ate up the beach on the last quarter.

I finished in a reasonable time, in the top 30 in a paper somewhere in Wales. The tide washed the footprints away. Memories are akin the torrent of the ocean, washing the past aside. In my forties, it was as if faded recollections of childhood never happened. Older became an obsession.

On July 31st 2009, Sir Bobby Robson died. He managed Ipswich Town through a golden period of success in the seventies and early eighties, an era I covered earlier. In the company of Alf Ramsey, a statue rests in honour of Bob outside the club's stadium. Though I never knew him, he was very much a part of our lives throughout my youth, before he left to manage England.

The next day I was in town and found myself at a flower stool. While I paused, my old mate from Maxie Fields appeared and for half an hour we spoke of the glory days. Stan acted somewhat embarrassed to buy flowers in my presence. Howbeit, in his Ipswich shirt, it was obvious where he was going. Before we went our separate ways, armed with a bunch of carnations, I wished him the best as he walked off without making a purchase.

Portman Road was half a mile away, but the car nearer. On the way home, I parked near the statue surrounded by tributes and tearful people paying their respects. On the drive homeward, I noticed Stan marching through Princes Street holding a floral tribute as if an Olympic torch. At that moment, I realised the power of belonging and identity.

Bobby was a Geordie, and on September 26th, his boyhood team he managed in later life visited Portman Road. Dozens of ex Ipswich players appeared before kick-off, to a round of applause. The tone changed when a voice of an angel rose from the pitch singing Sinatra's 'My Way'. Sat with my father and son, it was too much to bear.

Men cry, dance and sing at the football, while displaying emotions they dare not as a rule show in public. Yet thousands from Tyneside and Suffolk danced cried and chanted Bobbie's name, a genuine lover of the beautiful game. For we march on with no shame, and will be here tomorrow whether it be pain, tears or sorrow.

Sir Bob once quoted that a club is not the buildings, the directors or the employees. Nor is it the TV, and that other stuff, but the passion of pride and belonging. Now forty plus one, I was never so proud to be an Ipswich son.

Mind Games

Mile 18

'Flying high without a care, for a moment I succumb
to the beat surrender, inspired in tuneful thought.'

Mark Lankester

The runners high so good, yet hard to buy, served
in heart pumping strain. I edit a new order within
one's self to wipe life's stresses away, and on a blue
Monday in a world of confusion, genuine faith is a
sense of liberty.

Non-believers consider the tedium of pounding the
asphalt, or worse, the dreaded mill folly. The buzz
welcomed after training has more to do with the
minds subtle shift when in a realm of motion, and
those having discovered the power, celebrate the
blessing to one's spiritual vigour.

School was a universe of straight lines and rationale,
in an era of Rubik's Cube and Commodore 64.
Grateful the classroom had windows, I glanced
outside to escape boredom. Sunlight flickered through
the glass, raindrops spilled from the sky, and
rainbows shone a kaleidoscope of colours.

For we have two brains, well kind of. Neuronal fibres
connect the divided hemispheres, allowing them to

interact, akin to two computers wired up, to chat. The left-brain is the cynical governor who deals with decisions logically, and the right side is the more creative dreamer. Yin and yang that be seemingly opposite yet interconnected.

It is a documented fact that a range of people with injury to the linear thinking left sphere can despite that play musical instruments, draw and recite poetry flawlessly when the chilled out right is intact. For its function is more intuitive, spatially aware and spiritual, in tune with activities such as the arts, sport and music.

Endorphins a natural painkiller engulf the body when exercising and combined with the grey matters subtle shift to right sided dominance, people talk of the zone and oneness when everything flows. I run long to relish the phenomenon. The fretful left-hemisphere becomes a muffled voice, drowned out in a symphony of breathing life, akin to Obi-Wan Kenobi whispering to Luke to feel the force.

The dreamer muffles the logical sphere that reports tiredness as I jog for miles with a sixth sense that is primal yet so misunderstood, striding through the high trees and bluebell carpet of Brookhill Wood.

Yesterday I got up early to deliver the post and resolved to head out later, despite the body suggesting rest and an early night. The day not wasted when home, I drank coffee, threw on the Nikes and headed back on to the streets of no name to tread in solitary fame.

In pre-historic times, if a hunter got hurt or gave up, starvation threatened and adrenaline flowed until the pursuit was over and prey captured. Likewise, in war, soldiers are often oblivious to injury as the natural drug dulls the trauma.

With no battle to fight or food to find, I run. Meanwhile, long ago, the weary cave dweller ravished with hunger has a family to feed and runs towards a wildebeest. The animal charges and the hunter breaks a toe while retreating, spear in hand. Composure recovered Stone Age Man, is triumphant, and that evening ate a hearty feast. Only while relaxing does the foot throb and a seasoned warrior I doubt would cry or sob.

Present day, gliding for half an hour, deviating to the serene, dreamy right hemisphere, the worrier takes a backseat, ready to pounce to forewarn danger. Towards the end of the eight-mile spin, a meal awaits and full of endorphins, I write late into the night. Only the next morn, do I notice pains self-inflicted in the winter rains.

If stressed for lengthy periods with no release, mortals become sick. 'Fight and flight' syndrome in ancient times kicked in if attacked. This can be impractical in modern society. Instead, people have used drugs or alcohol to soothe stress that destroys if over indulged.

Glad I ran the world shone a sonic glow. The high the runner feels is free. If a pharmaceutical firm bottled and sold the buzz over the counter, I am sure that higher authorities might regard the life enhancer illegal.

Running helps relaxation and slumber. Sometimes we go to bed early, and cannot nod off, with the rational left in control thinking of ways to sleep. Instead, read a book, enjoy a film, strum a guitar and let the subconscious take a trip to the right brain, without thinking of the mundane.

Imagine staring at various upside down shapes on a blackboard, wondering which match. Spatial awareness works better when surrendering logic and using instinct. When in focus-surrender, everything fits as if by wizardry. Life is more than a science of predictability, and intellectual fools can complicate the simplicity.

England's football team has had trouble scoring penalties in tournaments. When in a stressed state and overthinking, the harder the task becomes. Matt Le Tissier, the laid-back maestro from Southampton, processed a lexicon of footballing skill. Howbeit, a multitude of experts considered the fellow unworthy, despite a fantastic penalty success rate.

Have you ever tried to think of somebody's name or place and then only much later does the answer randomly appears? The artistic right side dealt with the problem deep in the subconscious without us knowing. Scientists are seeking to figure out the marvels of the grey matter, and I wonder what side of the brain they use to research the magic.

Think outside the box, a friend once said, and I did just that on a football pitch, losing the ball without time to think. Words taken literally are the working of logic, yet miracles are born from dreams. Fuel for thought, umm I wonder, for I seldom practice what I preach.

When I was a kid, I picked at meals, yet in adulthood, I surmised running a licence to devour what I wanted. Boom, after a health check before turning 50, the perspective changed as I strode into the doctor's surgery in size 30 waist skinny jeans. Shock horror, cholesterol level higher than expected, I altered my diet soon after and fitness improved though boredom at meal times ensued.

Fact, running is an effective way to stay trim. Nevertheless, if we eat 500 calories a day, more than we burn off, we could gain a pound a week in weight. That does not sound much, but in the course of a year, a person could put on three to four stone, and that is worth consideration when retiring or taking a desk job after a physical one.

In my opinion, weight has more to do with calorie expenditure than intake. Not a mysterious science we need calories to survive, more if we exercise. The blueprint is the balance. Early Homo sapiens needed stamina to hunt, and human bodies have not changed one iota.

The body's compensates when starved and slows, as if putting a phone on economy to conserve battery. If a harsh winter, the cave dweller struggled to find food and when back to the norm, gained weight because the metabolism had slowed when in starvation. Modern day dieting is the same, so instead I prefer to exercise and eat in healthy moderation.

Muscle weighs more than fat and melts more calories. Carbohydrates such as bread, pasta, and potatoes are best before training akin to coal on a fire that burns for a long time. Carbs such as sugar flare providing a quick boost and protein such as eggs, beans, and meat are perfect for helping to rebuild strength.

Celebs plug diet and exercise DVD's for monitory gain and we become beguiled by fame. Ordinary folk can ill afford such luxury. For I say race through life, for food is mere fuel and not a treat while sat on a sofa seat. Read between the lines and gaze out of the window at the world of nature. For birds, live to eat or die, and fly without the novelty of thinking of what calorie count to buy.

Pride drives vanity to take up keep fit to alter the body's physique. By running to shed weight and pumping iron to build muscle, physical transformations can be dramatic, but the important thing is to change the person within ourselves.

Life encompasses all so many aspects, and if neglected will tumble like a pack of cards. For, dealing an ace is not a win and we must keep one up our sleeves. For no mortal has run a marathon entirely in the left hemisphere, gripped by the logic of fear. Faith in the future, what could go wrong, no spirit will fail if the heart stays strong.

C'est la vie

Mile 19

'The midlife crisis you're having at 30 is indulgent, but the midlife crisis you have at 45 is to an extent thrust upon you.'

Moby

If the rain falls, run and hide, and if the sun shines, slip into the shade and drink lemonade. Brits talk of the weather constantly, 2012, the wettest on record. The year a golden disc embossed with the phrase faster, higher and stronger, but only for a tad longer.

Yes, I am listening to the B-side of The Beatles Paperback Writer, furthermore cheers John for the opening line. The heavens have opened again, as I sit on the patio to write with a snail that roams nigh one's foot. The fragility of life resonates as I ponder, and if I had spurned a downward stare, the sluggard would have been a goner.

The earth spins on its axis whilst we strive and having scrawled a page, my friend has slithered two feet, and I detect a flock of tiny shells under a leaf. For every living thing has a spirit within to survive on a perilous slope, and I sense a warmth there is eternal hope.

The week after birthday 44, an epic duel raged once more in the guise of the Oxford and Cambridge boat race as the Thames shone a misty glow whilst dutiful men rowed in pursuit of victory. Yet strength and courage did not dictate pace, but a shattered oar and a saboteur who protested Dickensian spending cuts and the political elite.

Distrust of the establishment rose, and much as I appreciate the grandeur, I have more in common with the black cab drivers and working people that keep the streets clean and guard Her Majesty the Queen. Patriotism is part of a Brit's identity in whichever class should come to power, and to rob a soul of six months of training is a sin worthy of The Bloody Tower.

Londinium to the Romans, Lundenburg to Alfred the Great and Lundenwic to the Saxons, I am proud of the capital 70 miles west of home the envy of the world, rich in history, from the chime of Big Ben, that flows through the air, and the pigeons that live on Leicester Square.

The city has known grief yet continues to rise from the ashes, in a testament to what we are today. The pulsing heart of the nation forged in the spirit of so many races, the mecca of migration and the flag bearer of what is England. For I have stood on a dirty old river and watched the sunset on Waterloo with a London eye framing the view.

The Kingdom united for an Olympic party that summer to celebrate British culture for the first occasion since the Austerity Games of 1948. Britain had prepared for the spectacle for an eternity and having paid off the war debt to the USA, the country had the money to impress. Yet when ticketless, I thought c'est la vie, the Notting Hill Carnival was free, and boats and floats I hoped to see on Elizabeth's Diamond Jubilee.

The evening before venturing to the Royal Pageant, Junior and I ran the Kirton 5, a popular event hosted by Felixstowe Road Runners. Thus, the next day legs racked in lactic acid bore the brunt, as the bloody vessels passed painfully stood on the Embankment. Howbeit, the hordes arrived to applaud and wave in a rainstorm fit for only the brave.

In contrast, the sun shone to celebrate Caribbean culture in the Royal Borough of Kensington and Chelsea. The influence of the West Indian people is noteworthy, illuminated with vigour two miles south of Abbey Road. Beatle Paul sings as I write, and in tune with the melody, I hear Reggae. Desmond had a barrow in a marketplace, and Molly was a diva in a band, a detail I had missed for so long when listening to McCartney's song.

Pilgrims flock to savour the aura of tradition and Japanese tourists snapped as I danced a samba to the turned up bases amongst the surf of faces. For I am sure the folk from the country of the Samurai thought the scene hilarious, because the groove of a forty something can appear precarious.

Although I did not watch the Olympics live, the TV coverage of the opening ceremony inspired. I enjoyed the swift trip along the Thames, Isambard Kingdom

Brunel narrating the words of Shakespeare, and the Industrial revolution framed by the music of Elgar. For the global performance was the beating heart of Old Blighty in landscape, verse and tune.

Ghosts of great Britons shaped the UK, if not in invention but using weathered hands, with ploughed fields, roads paved and statues built. Touched with a tad of imperial guilt, a curious country rose from this pleasant land, burnt with coal and thumping steel that propelled the modern age with such zeal.

For me, the Olympian highlight was the 10,000 metres final. Mo Farah, a lad born in Somalia, spent his formative years as a refugee, and moved to England when a child. Now he represented Britain with the nation behind him. Yet number 13 visible on Mo's shorts, I feared his golden chain might jinx as he stormed to victory in what was an epic shot of glory.

The following morn, on a relaxing run into town, the right hemisphere of the brain took command reflecting the homeland I wander. The sign dangling from the Lord Nelson pub caught my attention because of the patchless Horatio. Hell, childhood ignorance on Maxie Fields was of no surprise, when even historians can only surmise.

Time waits for no mortal, plant or tear, and a younger man grew hungry to enter local five-mile events. So, marathon plans put on ice, I fed the benefit of fatherly advice. The boy's progress had been rapid, growing faster by the week, training on the rural expanse that is Suffolk.

Smugglers Pond is a favourite haunt in Rushmere St Andrew, near home. Folklore states that during the age of Dick Turpin, bootleggers submerged goods such as rum and brandy in the water to retrieve when the coast was clear, as safer to hide inland. Tea and lace, a likewise smuggled luxury, probably concealed within nearby bushes.

The neighbourhood we live would have been heathland in the 1700s. Though avoiding detection from customs officials was perilous, hiding places were aplenty. I think it probable that an ancestor took this passage to make a shilling or two when meeting a motley crew. Strange how after 50 years of being drawn to a seemingly insignificant spot, I have discovered the echo of mirrored reflection.

Unduly conscious of passaging time, after one particular run the lad and I noticed a fella feeding the ducks with his tiny son in tow. The scene could have been us, two decades previous, or Dad and I in the era of flairs and platform shoes. Generations change so fast, in stark contrast to the landscape that scarcely alters.

Training was fun, but as the months passed, some days I struggled. Whilst weaving trails and jumping gates, not once did we race, but there would come a time to set the pace. Yet for now, father and son strode forward, full of zeal never venturing far enough to become lost, before the onset of leafless trees and frost.

In the winter, I returned to distance training inviting a few friends to meet up at the Ship Inn Levington, close to where contraband laden boats landed in days of yore. The village rests on the banks of the River Orwell, prominent for locating fossils embedded in the clay cliffs washed from the riverbank. The scene leading to Felixstowe is sublime, with kingfishers and geese flocking to the marshy wetlands.

Unbeknown to my friends, I have a habit of taking wrong turns in life. I think the faith they had in me bore more from the fact I had been running considerably longer than they had and was intimate with the terrain. However, the paradox is I shaped the knowledge in a maze of confusion, and that day was another learning curve.

The four of us reached the edge of the docks and cut through the woods. Okay, if you enjoy a mystery tour. Surely, we were minutes away from a well-earned beer. When friends become fatigued and thirsty, bravado is the name of the game. Lost trees look the same wherever you are, and I prayed to find a guiding star.

On a road to nowhere, talking heads looked forward to their beds. Tired and after heaps of profanity, the pub appeared after 15 miles. Tom thanked me months later and kindly said with a sardonic grin the exhausting experience helped on his marathon venture with a few words I had to censor.

Often, if I fancied taking it easy and not wanting folk to note one's pace, I drove to a rural location. Nuffield Hospital is near to Brookhill Wood, where I can run for miles in woodland bliss with roving deer and the cascading creek for company.

One Sunday morn, after I run further than planned, I sat on a tree stump in the car park studying Garmin split times, before a voice calling one's name distracted. Stan on a flying visit to see his dad had pulled up in a flash motor. In contrast, I had toppled out of bed without brushing a comb across my head. While I drank a bottle of water, he lit a cigarette. The weed I quit when taking up running, but took to Nicorette Gum, trading one addiction for another.

For I chew today and recall popping a piece before the London Marathon. The familiarity while we gossiped was as if stepping into the kitchen to grab a brew and returning to revive a chat after a brief interlude. Yet since we last spoke, he had done well for himself, having moved abroad, apparently?

Time rolled on by and now 2013, we deliberated the demise of our footy team who had been in the second tier for 11 seasons. Manchester United again Premier League champions, I felt a pang of guilt he ditched the red scarf on the terraces when John Lennon was alive and Robsons boys began to thrive. Howbeit, he remained a steadfast blue.

The chairman Marcus Evans referred to our beloved team as a Cinderella club, and we agreed he bore little resemblance to Prince Charming. He had to stand and deliver, and when a long ball merchant arrived as manager, we were sceptical.

Thereafter we debated the merits of the recent Sweeney movie. The original popular whilst we wandered the streets of Castle Hill, the world was now as different as the film portrayed. Mark Kermode would have made a suitable case for the defence, but we just agreed it far from the best, and for a crime of cultural vandalism the director was a man to arrest.

I got hungry after chatting half an hour and feared the boss worrying I had gotten lost. The mobile phone as per usual sat at home on the dining room table, with a missed call while unavailable. Before disappearing, Stan eager to show off his wheels turned on the radio with a little less conversation.

So, it came to pass the reunion ended with an epic karaoke, echoing simpler times. Yet when he sped off, I realised the customised number plate that faded was Brother Joes Jaguar, that pumped out the cry of a superstar. I smiled and returned to my Ford Mondeo that failed to start. For a taxi out of the question, I had forgotten the phone, and it was time for a Basil Fawlty clone.

A few months thereafter, whilst in a bar in Greece, a text message read Stan was no more and four decades flashed by in seconds, as if a day in a life. There were few heroes left at 45. If he was Steve McQueen, the great escaper, I was the lesser-known Judd Taylor who threw him a baseball to take to the cooler. He represented the last link to those childhood days of footy, The King and Baggy Trousers.

Peter Pan no longer a hook knocked life sideways. An unnoticed face in the third row tells this yarn, with a zeal that takes every sweat and sinew from one's brow. Too ancient to be young and too youthful to cast asunder, one's story was ready to roll with thunder. Lost, midlife was waiting just round the corner as fate shuffled the pack and attacked, as I stood unarmed. For the moment I sought to climb back into the light, the cynical left-brain destroyed the rhyme.

With no thought of writing a book, and devoid of imagination, I opted to post depressing opinions on Facebook and pounded the treadmill with fury. Mourning youthful zest, I felt a quasi-teenage angst. Critics suggested I act my age, but life is no dress rehearsal, and I did not intend to fade to grey.

The day before my son's 18th birthday, we ran The Stowmarket Scenic Seven. Pre-race, we stood in silence and remembered those who had fallen in the horrors of war. The story has caught up if you recall chapter one. I had had a good life, for I would have been an olden in Viking times, and in a dash to the line, I prepared to pass on the baton.

For I know now I was not ready to yield. Nothing is over until we die. Yet regardless of how fast I ran, life went backwards and nostalgia became unhealthy. No longer striving forward, cast adrift as the younger generation took over, I treaded water as youth sailed off into the sunset.

Another year disappeared and aged 46 I attend a school reunion. On the way home, I rested on a wall in front of a house, leant back and toppled into a bush, unable to escape. Howbeit even in a drunken state, I knew a night in the shrubs was not an outstanding idea, and though the midlife crisis had begun, the scene was a perfect metaphor.

Abraham Lincoln once said I am not concerned you have fallen but the fact you have yet to rise to your feet, or words to that effect. For I fought on, despite knowing something was out of kilter. During this period, I suffered severe headaches. Howbeit prescribed pills by the doctor, they became less frequent.

Addicted to social media full of angst to tell, to log on quicker, I updated the Nokia Brick to feed a running addiction that used to be under control. Umpteen people had posted they were signing up for the Brighton Marathon. Despite the need for a rest, I entered. The distance and growing older I feared and planned the trip to be a swan song two days before one's 47th birth date.

Parkrun free throughout the land inspired, and the sport surged in popularity. Christchurch Park, a captivating place, evokes memories of childhood. The race is 5k, so trainers on I dashed there with gusto. The big turnout surprised. Times were a changing and the finish time popped up on the phone in an instant.

There were hundreds of pics taken, and one made the cover of this book. From that moment, I noticed cameras everywhere. Technology progressed, running moved on, but I sought to stay the same. The old days were less complicated when a rare photo appeared in the paper, and an age for results to arrive by post.

Life stalled, living on Facebook and checking updates. Someone somewhere had run longer and faster. Inspirational quotes leapt from the screen, and the mind never rested. The chicken and egg syndrome, was anxiety causing my migraines or the medication making me anxious?

Family life was wonderful, but times alone and in dreams were a fretful place and past haunted as if to remind I had not travel far from Maxie Fields, and had achieved so little. The waste of life is a sin. I wondered why I trundled on in mediocrity with nothing significant to offer.

By 2014, I was ill or injured. I hurt my back before a weekend in Yorkshire, and barely able to stand straight I ran the York 10k numbed with Ibuprofen fraught in pain. The rhyme and rhythm I lived by no longer worked, and the only motivation I had was anger. I fear I never recovered physically from that day forth, and the foolhardy stunt flicked a domino effect of injuries related to the body's core.

A 20-mile drive from our cottage, the traffic was grid locked and the chest and neck muscles tightened. When near to the start of the race, I parked in a side street and scampered along the road. Gasping for breath, with moments to spare, a Good Samaritan told me they had delayed the event for late arrivals. Fortunately, I had a phone and contacted one's better half, whom I had abandoned in haste.

Vikings landed in Britain to capture York in 866. During the race, I wondered how the Scandinavians shaped the accents of the crowd and nature. Yorkshire has a distinctive dialect and as I passed through the so quintessentially English city, I thought of folk suspicious of people they believe outsiders. If everybody traced his or her genealogy far enough, it would enlighten I think, or 'reckon' in Old Norse.

History radiates from every corner of England and much of my training takes me to the Martlesham Control Tower. The famous flying ace Douglas Badcr operated there during the Second World War. A housing estate devoured the airstrip in the seventies. Nevertheless, a pub stands on the village green in his honour that hosts an annual 10k.

Heroes don't wear capes, but this dude kinda did. He lost both legs in a crash, and a decade thereafter flew in the Battle of Britain. For shot from the sky and captured in occupied France, he escaped prison camps before seeing out the conflict in Colditz Castle.

A pillbox rests in Eagle Way and that year running the race suffering the aftermath of York, I noticed a kid sitting on the roof. I wondered if he knew of the historic significance, as I were unaware of debt we owed the few when playing soldiers on Maxie Fields in baggy trousers.

If he could overcome, one should reach for the sky. The search for the ultimate buzz turned into an addiction. Unable to let go, I ran further to seek the runners high I once took for granted in the mind numbing satisfaction of pushing the limits to regain the Holy Grail of youthful vitality.

Survival grew into a maze. The harder I tried to get back to where I once belonged, the more lost this middle age man became. Yet today I know the greatest gift God has given is choice. The devil kills dreams, and I resisted the temptation to share music with those who misunderstood ones lyrics.

Actions spoke louder than words, for I knew nobody cared if I failed. For I stepped out of the comfort zone and am no longer weak to see the light in what is the lord's unstoppable force. Practise a form of controlled failure feeds the eye of a tiger, and I seek it out and fail often. Reinvention thus made through trial and error.

I kicked myself when the world beat me down, and ultimately it was not the fear of inadequacy that crushed, but the thought of God giving me the strength I had neglected. Those internal words inspired and haunted for the next three years, and I did lose faith. Nor did I rhyme for a time, hitting the wall and a black tunnel that manifested its self into a marathon of attrition and an epic midlife crisis. For painting without emotion is a tree without roots.

Rise

Mile 20

'A state of flux between now and yore, youthful vigour on loan almost bleed, ones older self doth cry from yonder, your time is running out.'

Mark Lankester

The Brighton marathon I planned as the finale, in a hope of silencing the mournful Svengali. Face demons instead of retreat, for fading men should continue to strive. Old warriors of Norse dreamed of Valhalla, the modern eternal youth. The eyes, the window to the soul, sunglasses hid the strain. For suffer the silence, no one can hear.

Today I write in a better place and evoke a man who became a rhyme less scribe, beaming a light on the murky tunnel I floundered through in 2015. Now, torch in hand, I see the snags and recall the awkward passage of life's transition.

Anger is energy, and when building a mountain to climb devoid of positivity, there must be alternative fuel to fire the spirit. Though not wanting to train, I had no choice before youth ran aground. There are no second chances in life, and failure of no recourse, I needed a consuming distraction.

The avant-garde right sphere of intellect redundant, I called for linear thinking, ticking the required boxes to break 3 hours 45. The prospect of demolishing one's torso of no regard, for this was the last round of unvarnished enthusiasm. Christmas evening, the die cast in darkness, I wandered outside to the recycle bin, stumbled, and smacked the left shin on a wall in winter gloom. The pain searing I feared a fracture.

Boxing Day, I awoke and struggled to descend the stairs with the back injury incurred months earlier. The road to Brighton began with two black coffees, Ibuprofen, and an ice pack on the egg-shaped lump disfiguring the lower leg. The swelling persisted, and throughout training, I never sought professional advice.

Headphones on, I ran with Marshall Mathers, who spoke of having one shot in lyrical motivation. The palms sweaty and knees unsteady, I absorbed those words as if a disciple. Yet, calm and ready in cyberland, in reality I rope-a-doped ducking punches.

Rage drove the body on the solitary roads of Henley, Valley, Kesgrave, Heath, and Bixley and proved I could succeed, despite the death of the right sphere of dreams. Henceforth, I surged through the storm to pursue the footsteps of men and women who had stepped out in weathered shoes, fighting the same demons.

Depression I treated as a foe to conquer. Battles are there to win and though the mind pressed on the breaks, the limbs moved and the heart pumped the turbine. Nor did I have no notion how long the mood of melancholy might last, but survived the squall tied to the mask awaiting calmer waters.

Fifteen miles beaten on paved road, I sensed a wave of victorious satisfaction that the grey matter had carried the wilting frame. The finish time 2 hours 6 minutes 32 seconds on Ipswich streets. When home, endorphins flowing, I uploaded the distance on Facebook as the shin and lower back pulsated, reaching for Ibuprofen to numb the foe.

The Internet magnifies insecurity, and later I noticed people had run farther and faster that morn. Life imitates art, and often the poacher becomes the gamekeeper. Therefore, I too posted inspiring updates and posed for selfie snaps as if all was well in the world, seeking acceptance from peers.

The nemesis of social media can be a breeding ground for narcissism. Once a Greek fell in love with the face of reflection in a pool of water, and sycophants followed like lambs to the slaughter. If I said I had stormed a 10k with ease, was I extinguishing another's flame?

For if shining a light on one's self, we vainly project the photo shopped world of smoke and mirrors. In the pits of despair, smiling with thumbs aloft, people assume you have it made, and that is the living tragedy of bravado. So instead, I eventually posted failure for schadenfreude.

A friend noted I am a hard fellow to fathom. True, if sad I may dance a jig, and when fine sit in quiet anonymity. The mystery man we never knew, though we shared a brew. Social one week and silent the next, like you I bleed, one's book easier to read.

New Year's Day 12 mile planned, there was a parkrun at Kesgrave. Ergo, I jogged there, raced the route, and continue training. In this period, I watched old film noir movies, and played The Who album Quadrophenia endlessly. Jimmy the protagonist was a hopeless dancer and lost soul, and he too ventured to Brighton, in the year of 64 when the mods and rockers were at war.

One evening on the waterfront after running past The Lord Nelson Pub, I gazed out onto the river. I wondered if I could have been a contender and wished I had bought a guitar to strum the tune of Love Me Tender. Yes, the right side of the brain flickered on occasions when lost in motion, on what would have been Elvis Presley's 80th birthday.

Humanity chases the mirage, as if everything will be okay on arrival. Yet with a healthy family, I had struck gold. So what's it all about Alfie, getting up to run to the end of a rainbow in mud hills and rain for no monitory gain.

Today I can step back and surveyor midlife as if admiring a painting and notice details missed in the eye of a storm. Pals reached out, and I wasn't alone, but unreachable cast adrift in a lifeboat firing off rounds of ammo, regardless of friend or foe.

There were few races tougher than the Benfleet 15, and on a rocky slope with Father Time attempting to steal the baton, the walls were closing and bridges burnt. We take challenges because they are hard, not easy. Pain I needed, mind games and false hope of no consequence. So fit, yet weary, I ignored the brain to set out on mission insane.

A lad I knew from training for Brighton and entered the trail race. Methodical in method, he wanted to find a spot to simulate the expected hilly swamp. Capel Saint Mary near Dedham Vale suggested the scene of captivating paintings from the famed nineteenth-century artist John Constable.

Hence, the week before the Ben of Fleet I joined him in sub-zero temperatures. Alas, there had been a freeze. Dark setting out, we stuck to village streets until light before striding on to fields. The ground rock solid, trail shoes with deep tread were cumbersome. Howbeit, the 11 miles reaped confidence, and we continued thereafter on many a Sunday jaunt.

Benfleet, the stern test through the Hadleigh Downs, celebrating a 25th anniversary first launched in 1990, had built a formidable reputation. The night before rain fell, and I checked the weather summary for Essex, before adding duct tape to kit.

On January 18th, 2015, seven middle-aged guys posed for a group photograph before the epic undertaking, each had a story to tell and a reason to run in winter hell. For on a bleak day, under a sky of grey, faces shone a smile forged in noble guile.

The landscape desolate, a drone filmed from the air, never capturing the cruelty of the terrain. The beginning downhill, one ridge after another followed, folk crawling up the worst head to toe in muck, trainers loosened, with no thought of vanity, only survival.

The conditions eroded strength as if waves on a beach, the toughest a flat stretch between mile six and eight across marshland by the Canvey sea wall. Runners hit civilisation briefly at the local train station, where thick tread were hopeless, though an enormous edge out in the field where folk can yield.

I maintained a vertical stance throughout before leaping over a fella, as the finish appeared high above an incline. The race a true leveller, I doubt the most fleet of foot survived in plimsolls. Yet when halfway up a bloke tumbled, knocking one over, as we rolled to the bottom before racing to the top in mud-soaked glory.

Time 2:25:51 a club mate finished a few seconds behind and applauded me on pipping him to the peak. I admired his humility, because Ultra-Man ran 45 miles the day before in a feat I thought remarkable. The lonely trail I may seek, but tis a distance I fear and not for the weak.

The test was nothing to do with speed, but embracing nature in its truest form. Bud flung a beer on route to the car, for the first sip tasted of the elixir of life. Yet on the journey home, aching limbs forgotten, we talked football, as if the morning had been a garden stroll. The following day the back and disfigured shin begged for mercy.

Humbled and inspired by human spirit, many of those hardy souls were women. A detail I have neglected whilst writing. Until my late forties, preoccupied with what it was to be a bloke, strength I assumed the perquisite of the male. For the female of the species may say we stay kids for the rest of our lives, and in my defence, it is just how one's drive survives.

Post Benfleet, I worked out in the gym for two weeks to ease the impact on the lumbar region. Bill Conti's Rocky theme fuelled the stride before returning to the road for 14 miles. Confidence void, I never kept a training journal, as sure to disappoint, but have dates of runs planned and folk met.

The route to Woodbridge, sloping but enjoyable, draws one in as a migrating bird. Torso turned 180 degrees on return to Ipswich, the kneecap twisted to add to the body's woes. Howbeit on the climb out of the riverside town, the company of a pal eased the pain in the darkest moments of doubt.

February 8th, we drove to Great Bentley for a half marathon, start and finish on one of the largest village greens in England. Training had been light. Unprepared compared to peers, I set a target of sub 1 hour 40. Alcohol of no sin, a pint waited at the Plough Inn.

Time achieved with 43 seconds to spare, run in Essex biting air, I felt weary in body though charged in spirit. The footprints that lay behind on those winding lanes were God himself, who carried the frame of a man near lame.

For we are an eccentric breed, so far removed from the US of A where Rocky fought Apollo Creed, yet I understood the vocabulary of stubborn survival confronting such a rival, though mine were age and ailing speed.

Three Kings relaxed, toes warmed by a log fire watching football, surprised to be the only runners enjoying a beer. For calorie intake was of no fear as we talked of kicking a ball when younger and chewed the fat with hunger.

Arsenal five Villa nil, one more pint dear sir, there's time to kill. The green now deserted, 718 souls had run through the streets of personal goals. The afternoon a triumph despite excess, frowned upon today, by people devoid of grey. Over the hill, close to the summit, I had yet to tumble.

Cock a hoop with finishing in 1:39:17 the right hemisphere ignited the words of a beloved poet. Ray Davies sang of draught beer preservation in the English-speaking vernacular, in a world of village greens and class broken dreams. The Kinks frontman also wrote of a childhood friend, Walter, and how the boys planned to sail to sea when adults. Yet in maturity now strangers, only the writer's memory endured.

Ironically, later that week the song of lamented youth became reality, when I met Frank, the son of Ralph Coates, who recalled nothing of Maxie Fields. Never forget, for J. K. Rowling once declared old men are guilty if they do. Yet, though I was sad, he was still a blue, and his mum remembers me, Stan, and all the crew.

Edward Sheeran the famed musician sang wistfully of the castle on the hill in Framlingham, a place I know so well. Unbeknown to me, he once stood by my side whilst watching the local 10k. So humble sporting a cap, I knew nothing of the name and the songs that put him on the map. Thus, 'thinking out loud' tis a culture gap I had yet to bridge.

Ed supports the FA Cup winners of 78, and hears tales of gladiators of old when walking through the gate. For, I saw the Tractor Boys plough the field with skilful guile, and talk of the legend Kevin Beattie born in Carlisle.

The mind a dark place in mid-February, the spirit lifted when bumping into Kev at a local Newsagent. Heroes older and now so few, he gave up his time to talk of yester year, bringing a smile to ones face and so much cheer. Proud to shake the hand of the man who arm-wrestled Rambo into submission, the hero never shirked in the face of attrition.

Mileage increased and calamity hit during another long run, when the knee flared once more, Internet diagnosis suggested Iliotibial band syndrome. God, if this was to be a question of faith, the lord had thrown over a lofty cliff to scale, as if goading one to succumb to surrender. Doubt cast aside, spinning out of time, the soul were evergreen though limbs jaded.

So what next, my injured friend, February 22nd I travelled to Bury Saint Edmunds to run the Tarpley

20 mile. Fingers crossed, I prayed for the dodgy knee to hold for 3 hours. On arrival, although tense, smiling faces lifted one's spirits. For charity, I raised money for SENSE, and since kindly sending a running vest, I wore the gleaming tangerine attire in the race.

Half an hour before setting out, I noticed runners wearing energy gels on wastes as if ammo. Instead, I ate cake beforehand, followed by a fistful of painkillers and caffeine pills. Selfie taken with compadres, I am stunned I thought a photo of superior importance to limbering up before the distance of score.

Adrenaline charged, racing from the get go with pacing discarded, I hit the first mile in 7:56. Imagine, running a solid 14 miler, arrogantly disregarding the last six as a formality. For I saw club mate ahead, trod on the gas as the knee exploded.

Fate would have it that Jerry, who cycled past at the Stowmarket Scenic Seven, pulled up alongside once again to give faith as I jumped around on one foot. The guru urged me to continue and true to the pacemakers word discomfort subsided in conversation.

Mile 16, Jay rode off into the sunset to grant other's self-belief. Pain is information, and despite the strain when divine intervention rained, I finished in 2:51. For I were sure an angel would rise upon my shoulder as faith became bolder in the body now older.

Three weeks before the big day, I ran 20 in reasonable fettle with no injury woes, but days later caught a throat infection. The heart strong, I needed to close the next chapter on a high. Brighton the centre of the hurricane I could not escape, the script written.

Pragmatic in approach, physical condition aside, nothing would stop the mission I had to conquer. Imagine a car with a rattling engine, shot suspension, and wilting frame. For I awaited the credits to roll in film noir, the waves crashing on the beach, success claimed despite youth out of reach.

Saturday, 11th April, arriving at London by the sea, the enveloping white chalk bluffs and grand hotels conjured a picture postcard that is England. I frequented a hostel for two nights, a stone's throw from the pier. Once unpacked, I headed off to the expo to pick up race number 4083.

The hall was full of folk from Suffolk, including an injury-hit lad I knew from youth now reacquainted I had not expected to show. The hostels we stayed in backed on to each other and we chatted over coffee and pizza. Good to reminisce a test of endurance awaited the next morn, so we quit early with plenty of time to catch up post-race, with beer to taste.

Close to sunset, I took a stroll along the promenade, discovering Steve Ovett's statue on Madeira drive. In the Moscow Olympics, Brighton's finest won gold in the 800m, and his rival Sebastian Coe the 1500. For the titans legend survives for eternity, names linked as if gods floating through chariots of fire.

Twilight a mixture of emotions swept the soul, pausing in the effigy's presence, magnificent on a lofty plinth. Inspired, I relished the time alone. The inscription on the plaque read 'Steve Ovett Olympian', an epitaph to an athlete who lifted a nation. The waves kissed the beach, and I knew then, no goals were out of reach.

That night, unable to sleep, I studied social media with pictures of race numbers, fixed to vests with positive quotes. Migraine tablet swallowed, I stared at the ceiling, wondering why I was there, home with family, a happier place. The symphony bittersweet as one walked against the tide, to build a new order to rise again in search of Zen.

A spider crawled overhead as I lay on my bed, the movement a celebration of creation spinning a web. The clock struck twelve and still awake, marathon day here afeared at the trial I had to undertake.

Blue Monday's repetitive hypnotic beat helped the brain rest. So much so, I fell asleep listening to the rhythm. Alone, Gary Cooper at high noon without a Quadrophonic scooter, I intend to hurl the finishes medal from the white cliffs. For the long road not a glory hunt, but a purging of middle years, as if a caterpillar discovering wings moments before the fat lady   sings.

Brighton Marathon

Mile 21

'Can you see the real me...'

Peter Townshend

Marathon day April 12th 2015, I awoke to the harmony of seagulls and the band Royal Blood. One headphone hung from the ear, the music woven with ocean waves in foreboding menace. The Brighton rock duo had played whilst asleep and daydreams of a ten tonne skeleton dug deep.

The channel breeze swept the face through the window left ajar. So, with a yawn and brush of eyes, I walked over to close the rotting frame. A blackbird perched on the roof opposite stared back. Hey little creature, tell me what's on your mind. For the feathered friend appeared confused I was here, yellow beaked and sunken eyed a stone's throw from Palace Pier.

Brain fogged, the lump on leg gruesome, I felt rough with no hint of a laughter fit reading the prescription note the doctor writ. Fearful at what lurked behind the fated door, black coffee heaven sent, I wished to relax by the sea, tranquil and free.

On glancing through broken glass, The Wheel of Excellence stood with strength to spin an eye to nature's sky, with no sign of rounded sun. For on the birthday of Bobby Moore, West Ham and England's finest, there was no turning back until deed done.

Headphones on bracing to battle, Mike Kerr and Ben Thatcher duelled for dominance. How did we get so dark? For under pressure, I read into the lyrics, as if an inner voice were hailing a wind of change. Time running wild internal chat sped the heart, race prep more attuned to a mosh pit than a marathon.

I met my pal in reception, and we set out race bound. The weather was bright despite the chill, and Apollo rose shining on the march of humanity. On arrival, we saw elderly people sat on scooters, and Mini cars lining the streets. Mod vibe in the air, conditions were nigh on perfect for running.

The local green swarming as if at a rock festival, we greeted Suffolk folk readying for the journey, each with a story to share. Excitement in feet, I hoped not to fade before reaching the waterfront. Inspired, although physique torn asunder.

The human exodus of smiled profiles displayed no fear. For I can't explain the misgiving that scorched, as if coal to fire engine limbs. I saw no celebrities apart from Buzz Lightyear, but was aware Jenni Falconer was on the prowl, microphone in hand, as I prayed not to yield in a flustered last stand.

The elite field included Dominic Kangor, who broke the course record in 2013, and fellow Kenyan Eunice

231

Kales. While limbering up, I heard a girl mention that Jo Pavey was starting the event. The remark puzzled, until the penny dropped, English awash with double meaning. For the klaxon the legend pressed, dressed in her Sunday best.

Red corral found, and stood amongst the throng of 11,000, friends and strangers voiced concern over the state of one's leg. Comments brushed aside with a nonchalant shrug, sunglasses hid the truth. The minutes before the event, I marvelled. For no runner is a castaway, cheers rising from the masses, sunlit and shore so pretty, two towns, one city.

The horn blew, and we shuffled forward. Muscle memory suggested speed, though battered leg pulled on the brake as the knee, back and tendons ached. The first mile 8:41 of heart pumping fun, downhill into town we passed under a brick railway viaduct. Three friends in unity, a bond forged in spirit, as the paved path humbled.

Music pumped on passage to the Royal Pavilion, Indian in style and splendour. Mile 2 in 7:58 and on track, Simon the younger pulled away, lungs intact. The shin lump ready to detonate in Old Steine, I gestured to my mate of equal vintage with a knowing smile.

Scooters sped by, pursued by the Mini as we recouped seconds lost on the stride out. Pensioners traditionally enjoy weekends on the south coast, and today greying mods ride the Vespa and the Brit bike Lambretta. Small Faces going mobile, we weaved through the town before the highway widened on Grand Parade.

Kids in Italian suits caused havoc on the coast long ago, now woven into the fabric of Old Ocean's Bauble. Time a healer we redress the past painting out the cigar of Churchill and the cigarette of McCartney bare foot on a zebra crossing. For Queen Boudica torched London and today sculptured in bronze, she rises on Westminster Bridge.

The self-preservation of body and mind, I left pal behind on the coastal bluffs. Energy depleted, I extinguished unrealistic thoughts of a personal best. Yet, with the city out in force, the soul burnt bright, confidence lit in a foreboding flame.

On the tenth mile, along the seafront, the squawk of gulls above the crowd, plastic strewn across the path, Spiderman overtook, the heat rising, sunglasses in misted fog, Team Panda flag blowing a breeze as Boris the Spider strode with ease.

For a while, I chatted to a fellow my age who wore a Brighton and Hove Albion shirt. Spike spoke of Steve Foster, Jimmy Case and Michael Robinson and I lamented halcyon days of European glory united in two or three common languages, on approach to the Big Five Oh.

Halfway warm as a summer's day, carnival steel drums thumped with joy. The splendid Grand Hotel evoked the Bell Boy, and it's no secret affair Sting has since walked on the Moon. For grey hairs follow on a pilgrimage of youth, scooter'd and suited standing in the shadows where the in-crowd meet.

On route I snagged the odd orange when available, the sweet tart taste compared to gels exquisite. 'Tis a flat course, the experts said, although there were hills. The South Downs are no bowling green, the chalk cliffs vast and supreme cut from the ocean tide in Britannic verse.

The bulge on shin throbbed as if an external heart, strapped to the leg, heartbeats beating as one in blazing sun. Howbeit, Iliotibial band syndrome was still to surface. In the second half pace slipped, but passing the 20 mark in 2 hours 51, a 3:45 finish was achievable.

Willpower my loyalist friend caught up at mile 21, slapping the shoulder hard, the wind knocked from sails. The suffering dug deep, pain a temporary foe. Ibuprofen tablets dropped under foot with a shaky hand, endorphins and faith dragged the weary body forward.

At the Power station, with less support, we could have done with musical inspiration. So, feeling a trigger on a heartbeat pulling from an empty pocket, when turning the corner, I passed athletes coming the other way. Friends from home called out, and with a wave of an arm, I was too tired to shout.

Whilst I toiled in the latter miles, still here, trying to figure it out, Royal Blood circled the brain. The unique guitar style and driving drums triggered the spirit, as if I were the protagonist in a video of personal suffering, to which I found a banal comfort.

At mile 23, rows of beach huts stretched into the distance resembling coloured dominos. A fellow Ipswich runner caught up, and we chatted for a while before Billy Whoop sped off in the last 5k.

God did not design humans to run 42k, and warning signs ignored relying on faith alone I discovered the body's power cut. Giddy, with leaden limbs, every step torment, I glanced out on the ocean thinking just a Parkrun to go, searching for pious hope.

Heart on fire in danger of keeling over, embarrassed to struggle, a face in the crowded yelled beer. Cup hadeeth over, the clock ticking, I prayed for sub 4 hours. Feet of clay, I recalled the mud and hills of Benfleet, and months of training in a celebrated finale of a bittersweet symphony.

The stand along the home straight full of applauding onlookers, Steve Ovett's statue shone in reverence, one's rhythm skipping a beat in a Norman Wisdom tumble. Sunglasses on to veil the agony, I held fists up as if riding a scooter across the line. Finish time 3:54:53, within sight of the sea.

Brighton was a special test, not for kudos but deliverance suffering expected. The battle fought over the hill was a salvation that surpassed elation. The ending was not technicolour, but a black and white film noir V sign to the silver hairs that sprung from roots.

235

Medal earnt, winter days of training were a distant memory as darkness fled the soul in sun-kissed euphoria. When offered a foil blanket at the end, I refused, for I was not a casualty. Yes, I struck the wall, but that was a challenge conquered, faith restored.

Once composed, I picked up my goody bag and kit from the trailer. Energy drink in hand, I stumbled on to the beach amongst thousands enjoying the sunshine watching runners finish on a big screen. The ocean enticing, I waded in waist high to sooth the legs.

Whilst I people watched, excited screams and the shriek of gulls were indistinguishable. The darkness over, summer had arrived. Nice as the festival of human endurance was, I wanted a shower. Howbeit, the hostel was on the other side of the road, barriers lining the impassable Madeira Drive, the race still in progress.

Pondering the predicament, a familiar face appeared. Words of greeting one used, the lad polite though a tad confused, smiled thumbs aloft. Right here, right now, the name Fat Boy Slim registered.

Lost on an unfamiliar shore, the bright orange club vest was easy to spot. For there were a sizeable number of Suffolk folk who had descended on the Sussex town, enough to fill a local event. When mentioning I had seen a celebrity, I learnt Norman Cook lived in Hove and had run Brighton in 2010.

After enjoying the party atmosphere, sharing stories of highs and lows, I departed to find a loo. The initial thing noticed when gazing at mirrored reflection was the heavy bags under eyes. Tap water on face revitalised more than sugar-based drinks, and once sorted, the dark shades back on, and hostel bound I leapt the metal barrier when a gap appeared.

Inside four walls phone put on charge and screen display restored, I detected several missed calls. Bud had jumped the obstacle much earlier and eaten ready to hit the town for a beer or three. Twenty minutes later, after a shower and a Scooby snack, matey and I strolled up East Street.

The lad was in fine spirits, but had suffered on the streets. Tales of turmoil to share we called in on the Post & Telegraph pub. On a high, pint number one was as if drinking from the fountain of eternal youth and I craved a cigarette to boot. Marathoners stood out, medals and smiles a giveaway. United in satisfied pride we mingled with international voices of global English, on a brief stop of south coast cheer.

The face crimson and hair too short, one vowed to boycott the barber that has since moved to Birmingham. For, I reckon the cast of Peaky Blinders, now frequent the shop. 'Tis another gripe when older, though the temples grey and recede, vanity is not the prerequisite of the young.

Whilst resting at the bar, I noticed the lump on shin grew smaller by the hour. For the body knew the swelling that protected was no longer required. A curious case of nature I could not comprehend as the torso mended. Hydration needed, lager consumed at an alarming rate, I feared I would unravel in a dreadful state.

Hell, we could have remained in the pub all night. After six pints, I was sober, but rising from a comfy bar stool, the legs seized. On the agonising walk back, we passed a nightclub, and the doorman guessed we were marathoners. After 26.2 miles, the stairs were too steep to climb, though the brain danced a rhyme. Burger King sufficed, and relaxed with a coffee, I deflated as if a burst bouncy castle.

Monday morning I awoke fresh in mind, albeit tired. Yet to see the Queen of watering places in all its glory, I set out to walk off the aching limbs in search of a greasy spoon. The promenade almost deserted at 5am, and with less sleep than expected, adrenaline wove the body as if reborn.

The Brighton Pavilion made an impression. Later when watching the race highlights, I learnt that it was a makeshift hospital during The Great War. The building housed over 2000 wounded Indian troops who had been a vital part of the allied campaign.

Deep in thought, sat on the beach, I recalled Quadrophenia Jim hunched in turmoil. A youth not knowing where the road might lead, and I now a man destination arrived. The past an alien land, fashions and buildings alter, though not the human psyche.

The scooters revved, and a café I encountered by the lonely West Pier yet to die beneath the waves. The place a curious mix of runners, parka clad mods and bearded rockers. One lad asked if I had done the marathon, and where I bought the Fila Terrinda jacket. The latter of more interest to him, eighties casual vintage, a salute to one's youth.

Hunger pangs cured and limbs fuelled with caffeine I ventured to Preston Park, the name etched on stone. The walkways lined with pruned roses led to a dome-shaped café by a rounded lily pad pond. Engulfed in English Georgian splendour, rock music extinguished from brain, birds sang amongst the trees and suburban sky.

I could imagine Victorians in their Sunday best while I strolled in tracky bots as a visiting guest. For the scene was England in a simmer of hot steaming tea. A terracotta clock tower stood proud, and I noticed white lines drawn on the skies blue canvas in a blowtorch of metallic birds to and fro Gatwick and Heathrow.

The Chalet cafe appeared regal in architecture, blending with the nearby tennis courts. The building featured in the film 'The Chalk Garden' that echoes a notion tourists expect to find. Howbeit, a distant past that predates my time on this Island of class.

I ambled in feeling a scruff, and when ordering, the bubbly waitress assumed one was an Australian. The carrot cake delicious and moreish, when settling the bill she wished me luck on the trek back to Oz. Struve, I was too polite to correct the lass who once took a year out backpacking through Brisbane.

There is an Ipswich on the east coast of Queensland resting on the Bremer River, a former mining town.

Thousands of convicts from Suffolk are the forebears of the continent. The echoed voices mixed with an array of British and Irish dialects to form the sound of Terra Australis.

Victory saved from the jaws of defeat, the marathon was rewarding though not my swiftest. Youthful vigour is but a fleeting star in this sporting life. You cannot fall if never attempting to climb. The view is sublime if summit reached as the wood from the trees part in a panoramic display, hidden if locked in a tomb of fear.

The following morn I celebrated turning 47 with the love of family and reflected. For Brighton were the farthest I had travelled alone. The first day parted from one's wife in a quarter of a century. Half a man without a guiding light, lost in a crowd. The rest is propaganda discovered on the loneliness of the long-distance run. A thought inspired from the words of Sillitoe and ironed in a maiden of verse somewhere in time.

One Better Day

Mile 22

'Open water and clear of youth, I approached an aged
Isle, its banks a slippery slope.'

Mark Lankester

April 15th 2015 and in the night's midst,
dreamland is an alternate realm and mystical world
where the lines of realism blur daytime existence.
Barefoot on a beach somewhere in time, I see a
solitary boat centre stage wrapped in blue, soulless
without watering vitality to deliver motion. The tide
cruel, if tears from the heavens fill the hull, the
energy that gives will crush.

Open surf my biggest fear I tiptoe in, peddles biting
in sizzling seawater. In a flash, the land evaporates,
and the body plunges beneath the waves in a fight for
survival. A rope ladder swaying from the empty
vessel, a salvation, the power in arms I must find,
afraid to die, unable to fly.

The scene skips a rhythm. One is on deck, and a crow
in command perched on the ship's mask winks
approval. Two of God's creatures in glittering
sunlight, I was not the man I hoped to be, albeit

content with a sigh of relief to note the sea resembled an ice rink.

Act 2: the mood shifts, as if varnished in a wave of a brush from the fingers of Joseph Turner. A tsunami approaches mightier than Beachy Head, thunder in sky. Nowhere to hide, I face the foe, knowing defeat imminent. The ocean engulfs, and in the silence, I know the dream. Destiny controlled, a bluff scaled with ease I touch the Moon, and awake with plans to make.

Morning broke, and I rose a lion from the slumber, and whilst drinking coffee and toasting bread remembered the befuddlement of the unconscious. The ship had the name Shelley painted on the stern and his poetry I should learn. The night before I had listened to the sound affected vinyl of Paul Weller's Jam. Percy's words, inked on the sleeve, now understood chapter and verse.

Inspired, the heel aching, nature's warning ignored, I contemplated another crack at the marathon. The mind tainted with maramania suggested 2016 a different beast, if fit. Adrenaline, a friend, lies after races and within days I booked a sequel. For the capricious hand of fate neglected, a personal best was a cert.

If training mastered, a sub 3 hour 30 minutes was achievable a decade after London. Nothing was impossible with a year to prep, although injuries were of concern. There was not a second to waste, as if living stopped at 50, curved in carpet slippered feet.

The next day, I met a few pals for a social run organised by Suffolk Trail Runners, a self-navigating course leaving from the Limeburners Inn in Offton. So often I get lost, excuse the pun, and followed those more adept at map reading.

The English countryside jaunt brief, knee trouble returned and I quit after a mile, disappointed to miss the ruined castle where King Offa of Mercia once lived. The bonus was iliotibial band syndrome never surfaced at Brighton, only to strike walking distance from the pub with nothing at stake. So, with that thought, I ate and drank in the beer garden as happy as Larry Foley, a boxer never defeated and rewarded a grand in a pugilist's finale.

Two weeks thereafter wonky leg rested, I trekked round the Alton Water reservoir. The hills are a test framing the expanse and bobbing yachts. The right brain in control, I ran the trail twice to make 15 miles. Nor can I state why, though reminded of a party in days gone by at Tattingstone village hall.

The next weekend, the injury flared, wandering far from home searching for clues of Rome. So, apart from the odd outings, training ceased for several weeks. Instead, I sketched and read. Whilst reading I stumbled upon an article on East Bergholt born painter John Constable, who brought to life the scenery of Dedham Vale in the 1800s. The landscape protected by the Heritage trust recognisable to millennium eyes.

Flaming June arrived, and the mind inquisitive, I drove the 20-minute journey to discover The Hay

Wain oiled on canvas, the Mill, the view from Gun Hill and the splendour of the church of St Mary. Stour Valley River, a natural border divides Suffolk and Essex where visitors speak the rural lilt and Estuary English in equal measure.

The historical jaunt a hotchpotch of twisting trails, Flatford an impasse, cows blocked one's path, and I feared charging the Friesian Army. Howbeit, I stopped by later to see Willy Lott's Cottage frozen in time. The sky John captured in a brush stroke revered by meteorologists.

August 14th, the Ipswich Twilight 10k held on a glorious Friday evening drew top runners from afar, and son and I walked the short journey. On passage, we crossed Holywells Park, where Thomas Gainsborough sat with paint and easel before Constable's birth. History a ghost on every corner of the town I cherish, ridiculed by the discontent.

The event was a roaring success. The route took competitors past the statues of Bobby and Alf, the haunted streets of the Buttermarket, The Spread Eagle Inn, the cartoonist Giles sculpted in stone and the Swan Pub I once called home. Nor were memorials obvious. High above on the rear wall of the Mecca Bingo Hall a lone white brick honours a builder who died in a fall, a story forgotten in books of school.

October 21st 2015, a teenage Marty McFly arrived in a DeLorean from 1985, shocked to see one's older self. The same age, I now rattled out loops to Woodbridge, holding on to the youth that had since flown in the riverside town of one's injury woes.

Endorphins were flowing with a PB on Bundle Trundle bombing along Ropes Drive. What could go wrong?

Gravity is the killer. Tainted hearts heal, but to dive into the descending Sandy Lane when not in physical prime was foolish. Stupidity, the fatal flaw blew ambition as a twinge shot through the underside of the foot as if treading on a stone. Plantar fasciitis a condition common amongst runners affects a bunch of fibres linking heel to toe, thus endeth running for the rest of the year.

January 2016, training began with the news of David Bowie's death. For, dancing out of space with a limp, I headed out for distance runs, a dead man walking on the velvet underground of hope in Suffragette City. The Thin White Duke, an ally in sound and vision, nursed the discomfort of doubt.

The heel irritation lingered. So allowing the body chance to mend, I signed up for the Halstead and Essex Marathon held in May and dropped out of Brighton, music fuelling the bones through the Suffolk landscape. For a while, a pal joined in a marathoning pursuit, but he too succumbed to injury.

Permanent damaged feared, for months I doubted, sought medical advice and rested in ice. Several years thereafter, not 100 percent recovered, I carry on regardless, tendons tugging one stride at a time hand braking acceleration.

Throughout the spring, I extended my long run gradually, lungs unaffected from mechanical troubles,

Deep Heat gel warming the skin. The 20 miler arrived with birthday cards waiting unopened. Struve, 48 get a blooming move on mate!

Nike is the Goddess of speed. Yet in the left shoe, I placed a sponge to protect, having sought expert advice to no avail, heading out on a lonely trail. So, with nothing much to offer, I turned up Aladdin Sane, in a battle cry before sunrise. The detail of memory checked on Strava, the nursing of limbs today a palaver.

A perfect day temperature wise, the laughing gnome numbed the pain with the rain pouring on Purdis lane. Ten minutes in stumbling through the countryside, I spotted a budgie perched on a red post box. Umm, had the bird escaped? The parakeet can survive wild in the warmer climes of Suffolk, albeit damp and puddled.

The music of Ziggy Stardust played as if from the nest of singing birds. Goals are achievable whatever age, older another challenge. Bedazzled by the landscape, headphones slipped from ears to hear nature's cry, as I sped downhill into Brookhill Wood, vaulting a lying tree trunk on the tall trails.

The woodland a carpet of bluebells, I followed the Mill River weaving the boardwalks, the great outdoors beating the soulless experience of the gym. Mile three a brisk dash across Foxhall Road into Rushmere Heath, where I miss spent youth hunting for golf balls, evading capture from irate golfers and the hiding place of smugglers of old.

Kesgrave Millennium Jubilee Hall a welcome sight, I checked the pace that had lapsed on the lengthy climb out of Ipswich. Dogs ran wild, and relieved to return to the trees, the irritating sponge under heel I pulled from shoe to discarded helping to soak the morning dew.

Earlier, I mentioned Martlesham airfield used during the war and hunted for the airstrip overgrown and reclaimed by nature. Birds fly above and see our history etched in fields. Wingless I no longer run out of time, the Nemesis now an ally the heart pumped speed, whilst the brain preferred to learn and read.

The gallop downhill on route to Woodbridge helped the brief slump, the aroma of chips wafting from J's shop at Crown Point, with Pac-Man on the horizon. The yellow bin sits on a curve in the road, whence Stan sprayed a smiley face. Today the halfway mark hiding two energy gels. After swallowing one, I started the sharp climb towards Ipswich with the right side of the brain in control.

As foreseen, the last 10k was tough, but feeling strong, I had run a minute over three hours. The scamper through fields probing for relics of the past well spent, the journey through nature heaven sent, training was no longer a pursuit of sped but a state of mind and a chance to unwind. Howbeit, the decision to take a break from running for a week pre-race was a disaster.

Two days before Halstead, sick after a migraine, Saturday, I rested in bed and attempted to eat. On the big day, I awoke drained, drove the 33 miles to Essex,

247

and showed up in glorious sunshine. The hottest May on record, 600 runners turned out in weather perfect for sunbathing. Bravado is the cry of a fool and I was in no fit state to run a 10k, let alone a marathon.

Family travelled later and waited outside the King's Head pub with a supply of energy gels. Baz advised sunscreen, and I placed two drinks on a truck to take to mile 11 and 18. The rest is only my own meandering experience. Plenty of runners covered their faces in the white goo, and against my better judgement, I did likewise wearing sunglasses to confront the challenge.

Essex is flat, but Halstead was not. The moment the Klaxon blew, I knew I was in trouble. Chest tight after throwing up, I made a bold decision. If I was going to crash and burn, I may not finish, but a blowout was preferable than a slow death for the sake of an undeserved gleaming medal.

After a swift start, the pace pushed hard through Pebmarsh, praying for shade, the body pumped fountains of water. At four miles, my wife shocked at one's struggle handed over an energy gel. The hills never relented, and sunblock blinding vision I sought to rub the face with sticky palms, the Poundland glasses shattering at 10k.

Too fast, despite the conditions and on for a solid half marathon time at the next drink station, I asked for a cloth to wipe my eyes. None were available. The body overheating, faith melting the petrol level was on red. Still, I strode forward, hit halfway in 1 hour 43, and collapsed backwards onto the road. I fainted and for a few seconds, convinced a dog was urinating on me, anger fuelled the wilted frame. In fact, a chap was tipping water on my face. Eight, nine, ten, you're out...

Eleven miles from the finish I rose to feet with two options, walk or drop out. The latter accepted, I had work on Monday. The decision mulled over though never regretted. A white van appeared, and I flagged a lift. Today I am grateful to run. Over 600 set out and 452 picked up a medal. The race report coined the occasion a war of attrition. Umm, a bit strong, but mad dogs and Englishmen did venture in the blazing sun.

Mid-life was comparable to listening to a vinyl album dreading flipping over to hear the B- side older. For I had pursued the same goals since younger days, locked in the groove, refusing to let youth go, exhausted at trying to act and look under forty. The period from 2013 to 2016 the déjà vu years, as if watching a film I had seen before and knew the conclusion. The silent assassin age crept up, and the baton held for so long I discarded in a field in Halstead.

If judging someone, remember we have lived one life. When at a race, we pick out rivals in shoes we have never trodden, diverse in lifestyle and unique in ability. The nemesis on track and trail may have endured adversity just to be there. The start line staggered, and path rocky.

This book has been cathartic. Older threw up so many emotions. In an earlier chapter, I addressed an eating problem as a teenager and kept the subject as brief as possible. Dark clouds coincided with adolescence and mid-life, but I have manic phases where I am energetic and sociable, and times when motivation is a struggle.

When a boy sometimes instead of playing football with mates, I sat and spectated from a distance, alone in thought, observing character traits. Then, after a few days, I would snap out of the gloom and yell for the ball. For, I was taking a step back before returning to the narrative. While I write this book, I will be away from the field of play for longer.

Long ago, experts regarded nostalgia as a mental illness linked to depression. Umm, I am uncertain, but I do not think dwelling helps. The best day is today, but then I worried over everything. A slight palpation I feared I might die, and now the colours of the rainbow I notice in the sky appreciating the small things missed when in such a hurry.

Every two-year footballing madness strikes and the summer of 2016 were no different. Viking raiders humbled England, and once again, we mourned. Who do we think we are, superstars, oh right you are? For we shone like the moon, the stars, and the sun and Iceland had us on the run. Warriors of old defeating men softened by gold.

Time for a holiday in Italy, the land of the Vespa and Latin, we flew to Lake Garda, with sights to see. Sugg's autobiography read on flight and impressed by the self-written yarn, Graham had lived a life with a story to tell at 50. Inspired, I wondered if I had the words to hand to scribe a tale. God loves a trier, no fire lit without a strike of a match.

Unable to relax, every few minutes cabin crew asked if I needed everything bar peace. Kids were yelling, folk kept getting up for the loo, and the pilot interrupted to state we were flying at 20,000 feet. Paperback given up and placed under seat, I tuned into The Beatles. People and places remembered in my life, a seed of change swept the brain.

While I was out training in Lake Garda, I joined a Sicilian jogging the same route. Stefano spoke little English and mentioned his love of running, and only later did I understand with a phrase guide in hand. For, as we ran up the steep slopes, and took in the splendido scenario at the start of a new day, I knew where   my   destiny   lay.

Paperback Writer

Mile 23

'For an Englishmen never retires, he just changes,
returns and stands back and admires.'

Mark Lankester

January 20th 2017, listening to the news suffering
ole rag blues, the pencil on easel produced a fellow
that looked a weasel. The Latin foot of plantar
fasciitis had become part of life. Experts advised rest,
and weeks and then months passed as I sought other
hobbies to pursue.

I gave up the faith in false prophets and searched for
solace in benevolence. Once more, I drew and a face
emerged of a dinosaur who would stare across the
pond for four years or more. Reality had become a
parody, and the one world that made sense existed
safely in the mind, drawn out in ink when ready.

In the spring, having not raced for 5 months, I tied on
the Nike's for three short pre-entered events. A train
less man devoid of fitness, hoping nobody was there
to witness, the race Little Bromley ended in a
churchyard cemetery, Kesgrave was a rave and
Colchester finished on a track where once the

Romans attacked. All so English, tea, cake and chatter, times did not matter.

The eminent author, George Orwell, famous in the last century, spent much of his life in the seaside town of Southwold. On a visit, I spotted many of his quotes painted on the wall of the pier. One changed my destiny, noting our differing personas and allegiance to the Almighty living on an island we call Old Blighty.

I love the Britannic tribes and forgotten scribes, and whenever abroad, I miss home. Once our plane reaches these shores, I stare out at our green and rain swept land. Darkness faded on the sands of Lowestoft, when recalling an Orwellian quote. For reality exists nowhere else but the heart.

The heel of tenderness softened by a rubber sole, had given me optimum to pick up a pen and roll. For on June 19th Brian Cant died, age 83, an Ipswich lad the same as me, and I recalled childhood and him narrating Chigley and Trumpton. Ibuprofen dulling the pain, it was now time to use the brain.

I was 49 by the summer and returned to running, tuning in to a rocking band. Acoustics stripped bare, the seed of change floated in my mind once again as we flew to Italy. Sorrento is on the south-west coast, and on route, we roamed through Naples, where the Hand of God shines from murals throughout.

Maradona adopted the city in my youth landing as a messiah from footballing heaven, 75,000 souls descended on Stadio San Paolo to witness. True, the rascal robbed England of unlikely World Cup glory. Yet, I wanted to hail when the cosmic kite danced round Suffolk Boy Terry Butcher and half the team to score a blinder. History played out in a Shakespearean twist as the stiff upper lip tightened in reverence. For an Englishman could never applaud.

Saddened by the decline of heroes, I talk of aging throughout this story. For disciples put them on a pedestal from which they fall. Diego akin to George Best was a genius, but a man flawed and mortal. Forget a statue worshiped, appreciate their fleeting gift, and respect the older incarnation, for his youth rests in a land of memory. Nor should life after fame dampen their eternal flame.

Our hotel situated halfway up a cliff with a rock face blocking the balcony view, we headed out to explore, descending the steep steps into a maze of alleyways. For it wasn't until I reached the waterfront and inhaled the sea air the holiday had begun. The aroma of coffee wafting before temperatures rose, early dawn runs into town, I relished.

While in the country of the Latins, we visited ancient Pompeii. The volcano Mount Vesuvius erupted in AD 79 and buried the Roman city under ash and lava for 1700 years. For it's an irony that in 1943, allied forces bombed the ruins. A modern, lonely statue struck my gaze on display amongst stone buildings. The survivor inspired a sketch that was to be this book's front cover, but I felt it might confuse reflecting a historical history of Rome.

At school I wondered what the point of learning Latin was, an extinct language brought to the shores of Britain by the Romans. Ergo, half the names and phrases together with Greek are in common use, if not recognisably similar. Plantar Fascia is a de facto bona fide pain in the ass. Tempus otii, it's time for a coffee break and a blast of Status Quo, I think.

Once home, the book took shape and became a priority, but weeks later I attended yet another paid up jaunt. Sunday August 6th at the Norwich 10k, on a bright sunny day, aficionados introduced Canaries legend Grant Holt to the crowd. Runners cheered and smiled in our direction as two Tractor Boys and I stood, arms folded, unimpressed, wearing Ipswich JAFFA orange.

The rivalry between the East Anglian football clubs intense, I appreciate how we can wind up Norfolk folk. The glory of ITFC long since gone, a yellow canary asked if it bore me watching old victories on Pathe news. Dear John, technicolour dreams are not forgotten.

I have to say I enjoyed the outing despite the hills. Six thousand ran in a carnival atmosphere that rivalled any marathon. Sky of blue and sun beating, we battled the heat passing the city's landmarks to finish at city hall. For the black veils of melancholy, a distant memory, and thirsty work in search of the fourth chord, it was a perfect remedy.

No watch required I had become more preoccupied with rhyme than passaging time. Although on checking results, I had kept a sub 8-minute mile throughout. The goody bag fruitful contained a chocolate treat, a can of Adam's Ghost ship from the Southwold brewery and a snood soon to prove useful. My pal was not so fortunate and received a Norwich City scarf.

August 16th and it was now 40 years since Elvis died, and Castle Hill seemed another life of baggy trousers and the misunderstood. For it is a lifetime study to find out who you are and for several weeks training ceased, as I wrote energetically disappearing from Strava.

The Felixstowe Coastal 10M in September was the racing finale. Stood on the promenade, I thought of my first event there 20 years earlier. Far less fit and lacking speed, I'd have sooner sat on the beach with a book to read. Hot, I suffered, though a joy to see smiling faces.

Later, studying the photos, I noted the old pier, once the grandest in England. During the Second World War, shortened because of the risk of invasion, the wooden jetty looked good after recent restoration. For an Englishman never retires, he just changes, returns, and stands back and admires.

William Shakespeare suggested a wise man knows he's a fool. The word 'Great' a heavy cross for Brits to bear, we are a curious nation that celebrates defeat. For Rudyard Kipling preferred to treat success and failure the same, and Monty Python mocked our stiff upper lip. To talk of innermost thoughts is difficult, but writing cathartic pen to page the words flow. Men have written of angst for generations.

One evening my wife and I watched the Christopher Nolan movie 'Dunkirk', a masterpiece of suspense narrating a tale of survival and faith in the face of overwhelming odds. No longer a kid, and now a father witnessing the squander of precious youth, I remembered Grandad's tales and my fear of the sea. The ocean draws me close, as if placing a finger to a flame. I felt guilt, mid-life had hit. Lest we forget, for how fortuitous was I to grow older.

Two years had passed since the foot injury. The less I ran, the more I wrote of a runner in tandem with the onset of middle age, splashing a dab of nostalgia on every page. I planned a year to complete this project, which ended up four. Few knew of what I had undertaken as I faded from the social scene.

Great Run Local is a free 5k event held on Sunday mornings. The atmosphere relaxed and friendly, organised by volunteers throughout the UK. Yep, a few speeds freaks show up, but the aim is to promote a healthy lifestyle. Inspired and now an absolute beginner, I gave it a go. History a page long since read the future yet written, change an opportunity to discover fresh horizons.

Whilst writing I listen to various artists to set the imagination aglow and for this chapter I dug Bowie and the Quo. Older than a new dawn, many musicians play pub gigs for sheer joy when fame wanes. We can learn from that. Ziggy played his left hand, as did Macca, though Spitfire did not approve.

The most ferocious competitor's veterans, a friend used to win a wealth of races, before Father Time called last orders. The old warrior continued the fight, as younger men rose to challenge. Once he joined the middle of the field in a community five miler, as runners aware of his past sought to dethrone the king. Sad to say, Rick invariably travelled miles to seek anonymity.

These guys are hard on themselves, thinking self-doubt a weakness having spent their entire life strong. Talk and grab a chink of light. There is always a better day! Howbeit, a friend new to running lay down the gauntlet at Needham Lake.

Lack of training and injury is of no consequence, excuses ignored, challenge issued, I had no choice. That morn, limping through the finish line, I carried on into the countryside pondering this story as voices faded into the distance.

Planta fasciitis manageable at a steady pace, yet another mate entered his first race. So in moral support I signed up for the half marathon organised by 'Inspire Races', on the Snetterton motor racing track. Apart from a couple of bridges, the three lap course is flat, fast and traffic free, built on the former airfield used during World War Two.

September 19th, eight weeks before the big day, I hit the road to check fitness and thereafter ran regular 10 milers. The workout aptly named 'Nostalgia' dated October 1st survives on Strava. I passed my old house, school and park where I grew up as a child and that afternoon wrote the chapter 'Castle Hill' as the head churned ideas, the lower leg ache a constant.

November 19th we arrived at Snetterton, the winds high and icy cold, the winter sun shining in sky. Seven decades since the war, I pictured the American B17 bombers taking off from the flat landscape, over a tapestry of agricultural fields of many colours. The organisers had allowed headphones. Pleased, I made a playlist in advance.

I noticed an old classmate limbering up in the aircraft hangar and sauntered over to him. Once in an English lesson Dave gave a comical speech about his life as a 'rude boy' sporting a pork-pie hat and skinny tie. He asked if I was attending the next school reunion. The answer no, the past a foreign land, I had learnt another language.

While warming up, I talked to a heavily bandaged fella doctors had advised to give up the ghost. For when I enquired how he coped with the disability his reply I found inspirational, and in a state of acquiesce plugged into Oasis, to await the sound of the starting gun.

The left calf hurt on the tarmac designed for the heavy use of motor racing, but loosened at mile 4 as the wind whipped hard across the track, drowning out the cries of Liam Gallagher. Every time my feet struck the ground, perfect for those hunting fast times, I noted the advice the battle weary runner had given on the start line. Pain is information.

Many of the turns and straights had the names of famous drivers. Little do I know about motor sports and wondered if the bend called Nelson was a reference to the British sea faring legend born in

Norfolk. Bomb Hole Corner, a point of interest, was not bombed during the war. Competitors call the narrow turn bumhole because of the danger, and the wording bowdlerised so as not to offend.

The second lap, I pushed hard with the advice in mind from the bandaged warrior, together with motivational songs helping to propel the body forward. When I hit 5 miles, I knew there was an hour of discomfort ahead and sped up, regardless. The Beatles drove the legs along Senna Straight, and by mile nine Ringo had blisters on his fingers. The song recorded the year of my birth would have significance 24 hours later.

Born to run with a ticket to ride breathing in the cold air, I clocked 1 hour 46. Years ago, I ran much faster, but thanks to the power of positivity I was back on track with Phil Lynott on attack, the foot slightly out of kilter, with the odd swear word under the breath I had to filter.

When finished, I noticed a giant red deck chair and my pal took a picture of me, sitting a little man reborn. Great East Run used the image in an article about this book. Yep, the written marathon was long, albeit rewarding. The morning after, hardly able to walk, I turned on the TV. A psycho was dead and the words Helter Skelter I read.

Looking through a glass onion, I at last decided contact a physiotherapist. The discovery of scar tissue inside my left calf was of no surprise as I had often ignored warning signs. Acupuncture helped, albeit briefly. To be Frank, I visited the surgery a few times, but the leg is permanently caput. No matter, we carry on regardless.

I hadn't planned another run as Christmas approached, my busiest time at work. Yet, while browsing the Internet, I found there was a half marathon trial race at the Kings Forest near Thetford named after King George V. The festive challenge would end the year nicely. The BBC filmed Dad's Army nearby, tall trees lining the route, I expected to see Corporal Jones in a panic.

The event was the perfect trail run, reminiscent of the New Forest. As I composed this book, I wrote in actual time drafting this chapter that evening. Rural running I love, for in a curious case of body and mind my age now fitted like a glove.

The pressure off, I showed up bearded, wearing a hat in anonymity. Before the event, shivering impatiently, I spotted a pal. Just as I was about to reveal my disguise, the horn blew and off we dashed as I exhaled a mist that fascinated me as a kid. Icy, I struggled to keep my footing passing Lark River, the crunch of sleet underfoot. For speed hit the tracks, for an experience embrace the trails.

A lad in Santa attire caught up with me, spotting a long red beard. The outfit must have slowed him somewhat. After a few miles, I introduced myself, and we chatted for half an hour, skipping through the snow. Everybody has a unique tale. People's stories fascinate, for some were serious drinkers, drug abusers and plain unhealthy before turning a corner.

Dan ran for charity, I can't recall which. He put some effort in, and for his benefit, I told him the pace too fast. At mile nine, I suggested he push on ahead. Instead, he staggered off for a pee as if a tipsy Santa. So here it was, everybody having fun, mist on breath below distant sun.

Nose running faster than I run, fingers numb, I pulled sleeves over hands. The pines protected resembling festive trees with snow hanging from leaves. Once the largest forest in England, most were high and planted in straight lines. The course, whilst listening to a band on the run, a tad further than 13.1 miles was a pleasure.

Back at the car, phone ready to snap a selfie, the older profile appeared on screen. The moisture on the tips of the beard shone grey. I no longer cared. The pressure of fighting lost youth spared the outlook bright, aging was of no consequence.

Travelling home, Elvis played on the radio, still inspiring the mind. For his echo has been a constant in my life. Strong winds blow away doubtful fear, as long as we harness the strength to dream. Nigh on 50 years on planet blue, the future was a beckoning candle half written, but ready to redeem the soul and fly!

Inspired

Mile 24

'Suffolk rain on green fields, floods a passion in my
heart that never yields.'

Mark Lankester

New Year's Eve, sat watching festive TV
awaiting 2018, I suggested a trip in the car,
destination a surprise. On passage, the streetlights
morphed to trees against a blackened sky. In a state of
sobriety, on arrival, we parked at Woodbridge station.
The Anchor alehouse overflowed with singing
revellers and not wishing to run the gauntlet we
slipped past The Riverside Restaurant and Theatre in
shadowed anonymity.

Hogmanay on the riverbank I hoped to be romantic,
as we walked over the railway bridge to the water's
edge enveloped in black. Sense of sound a guide, the
howls of wildlife drowned out distant karaoke. The
town behind lit in pastel and the countryside far from
peaceful, the cry of barking foxes, badgers, and deer
rang a sinister symphony.

Yes, I worried one's better half, but she kept quiet, as
I appeared to know where I was going, discovering a
bench overlooking the estuary. My heart lifted to see

shadows of others, as we stared in complete darkness over the water where Raedwald, the Anglo-Saxon king, supposedly rests undisturbed.

The mist eerie, the backing track of nature a lull before human celebration, blackbirds sang in the dead of night, whilst we huddled together in anticipation. When the clock struck 12, fireworks exploded from either side of the bank, boats framed in a pink glow as the horizon shuddered. The Deben River at midnight an exquisite sight I thanked the Almighty for one more year.

The next day, I awoke restless, Sky News showing much of the USA locked in ice with frozen sharks washed up on beaches. Here, we had the usual rainfall, but with gritted teeth, it was warm enough for a tee shirt. For, on the rare occasion snow lands, Suffolk comes to a standstill.

Car keys tucked in hand, watch discarded, I returned to Woodbridge for a run through time, taking in the view. For early morn January 1st, I had checked the tide, the passage free through Kyson Point where once I had to wade for safety.

No need for artificial soundtracks to pump the heart, songs of nature filled life-giving air. Yachts glued in mud as if statues, ducks and birds waddled and pecked for rich picking brought in land from the sea. For, from darkness to light, I saw the orchestral swirl that sang in another year that revellers missed in festive cheer.

The night before, I caught part of a gangster movie. The climatic shoot out played on my mind. Eliot Ness stood in Chicago Union Station, a menacing presence in the air whilst a mum with a baby in a pram, unaware she had walked into a stakeout, struggled laden with belongings. The epic scene set in the 1930s America, for me a metaphor to motherhood, the fragility of life and survival.

Mother Nature gives birth and nurtures. The self-destruct button pressed by man, the female of the species having no such luxury, is the other half of the sky when alpha males cry forever in their debt, emotions mixed with thoughtlessness. Remember, when taking on dangerous pursuits, someone may have to catch your fall. Okay Mark lesson endeth, no wading through tidal waters.

Burnt out cardboard tubes attached to wooden sticks was the only litter scattered upon rustic floor, the wind cutting across the river glistening like a mirror into watering eyes, that winced on passage to a sunlit sky. I wondered how far a firework could travel and imagined Roman Ships of old appearing on the Deben to bring civilisation, word, road and distance to the land as I turned to head back whence I came.

On arrival at Sutton Hoo, mounds rose from grass to celebrate buried Kings. I trod with respect, for who knows what lays underneath undiscovered resting in peace. The discovery of the medieval Long Ship in 1939, had evaded spades 1200 years or more, 86 feet of wooden frame lost in acidic soil sent forth to heavenly sky, although a lady birds shell survived and a rich botty of gold, silver, a sword of a left-handed mortal his imprint intact.

A decade later, archaeologist Basil Brown now famed resumed his passion and excavated Castle Hill on which they built an estate where I lived as a child, pottering bucket and spade in the back garden digging for treasure unknowingly upon a Roman legacy. Modern mixed with old my Action Man figure rests amongst broken clay and so to Basils daughter's roller skate that fell into a ship's hull long since decayed.

It felt invasive striding through a historical site, as if weaving a cemetery, the distance of time irrelevant. Beyond the water, we saw the bench in which we sat the night before, listening to natures cry over Saxon fields that thrived before Norman Conquest. The brutal dictatorship locked Old Blighty in the vice of class we never fully relinquished.

For almost one thousand years, most invaders have failed to plunder these shores, the English Channel a natural defence. Howbeit, with human invention a tool of destruction, Zeppelins descended on Suffolk's Kings Lynn and Great Yarmouth to drop bombs, and not since Rolls-Royce Merlin engines ruled the skies has an Earthling tried to claim our fields.

Rendlesham Forest where doves fly, childhood memories returned of visitors from the sky, as I trundled forth, forgetting distance tread, with legs scratched from trees that itched and bled. A fellow in a wood with multi-coloured mirror perhaps, for if an

266

alien walked this land, days of yore had a passing hand.

Happiness: a warm gun, a man in boots lying with his hands working overtime, might one day find a soap impression he made donated to the National Trust. We are history walking as if a lizard on a windowpane.

Umm, I have heard there are plans to make two movies set in Suffolk, 'The Dig' recounting the events of Sutton Hoo and 'Yesterday' featuring the melody of the Beatles. If they require an extra that speaks a rural tongue, I am available, for there are places I remember, though some have changed.

The mind wandered on the long winding trail, and by mile 12, I almost forgot I was running, endorphins flooding the body. The Imagination dominated, with the left hemisphere of logic ready to take control if I tumbled. Nobodies snuff out prophets, but written word and song roll on not silenced. History, our legacy, what went before us around every corner.

The river rested on my right on return, as I summoned up the fight weighed down in mud, out running the incoming tide that rose as if a filling bath tub. I had cut it fine and passed through Kyson's Point, the land a narrow strip, a twist and a climb towards fields of green and cows sipping from a shallow stream.

The last stretch was difficult as I weaved on coming dog walkers and folk flooding the walkway, ankles taking the brunt, sloping grass on either side. A quick dash across the railway track to the tennis courts and coffee shop, I staggered to Cherry Tree Lane to where my warm wheeled chariot awaited.

Bearded and dishevelled I stared into the car wing mirror, a butterfly catching my eye. Rare to see a fluttering symbol of resurrection that time of year, I also saw a light bulb dead on ground, shining through reflected sun, a sign of redemption and a rebirth of hope.

The first week of January, I logged 35 miles, staying in shape easier than fighting to reclaim. However, as the lungs drove the body forward, the dodgy leg was payback for the folly of youth. Howbeit, the comeback had started positively with ears wired to British guitar strumming poets.

Back at Snetterton race track on the 14th, surprised to run 7.40 pace for 10k, I set a target to hit, booking two half marathons for the spring, Stowmarket and Colchester. The heart grew stronger throughout the winter, running the trails of Alton Water, and the younger I felt the greyer the beard became.

Saturday, March 3rd 2018, I began shaving, listening to the radio, my profile rounder as the greying hair disappeared. Face half sheared, I heard that the first mortal to run a mile within four-minute fleet of foot had died. Roger Bannister started university shortly after the Second World War, many of his forbears losing their lives in the conflict. Too young to serve, perhaps he thought it his duty to strive for greatest.

The phrase 'rest in peace' derives from the Latin term 'requiescat in pace' and is a perfect tribute. For people assumed it impossible for a human to accomplish such a feat. He studied neurology, training hard between walking the hospital wards, while athletics abroad were already adopting a professional attitude, Wes Santee from the USA, and Aussie John Landy, his chief rivals.

Elvis yet to rock these shores, the Oxford Flyer took to a cinder track. The fickle British weather a worry, he had studied the function of the brain and must have realised his mind was his biggest hurdle. The attempt in doubt just before the race he looked out onto a church spire, its flag no longer fluttering in the wind, sun emerging from a stratus sky. Gods sign, he set out to redeem his soul and fly.

Two friends supported him as pacers, one of whom later co-founded the London Marathon. When he sailed over the line, collapsing into a joyful crowd, the country awaited the recorded time. For as soon as Norris McWhirter uttered the number three, the door of possibility opened for others to follow, 24 athletes breaking the barrier within a year.

The day after the sad news and inspired, I undertook the mile on the track, home of Ipswich Jaffa. The weather favourable I left the house wearing an ordinary watch, with no point in tracking progress by GPS, jogging there as a warm-up. For we say curiosity killed the cat.

The run took in the scenic trail of Rushmere Heath where I ran cross-country at school, thinking it torture often hiding in bushes to miss a lap. A mile from the sports centre, I passed the church where we married.

Churches in picturesque villages are familiar in rural England, and at stages, it could have been May 6th 1954 on route to Iffley Road.

A distant chime of bells signalling Christian pray, the song by naked eyes rang true in my mind, for there was always something to remind me, every step I strode. Muster your courage, run the spectacular wall, my intonation of Suffolk words peculiar. No longer young but with the world beneath my feet, I thanked fate that gave me life so precious.

When I arrived, having warmed up for half an hour on route, I ran hard round the track and struggled within 200 metres, Yogi jumping on one's shoulder. On the second lap, the lungs hurt and on the third, I prayed. The thousand paces a tad under 6 minutes I felt a fraud. Albeit, Sir Rog, the scientific expert in the working of the old grey matter, had given me heart.

Mid-March, the Beast from the East hit, entombing the entire country in a blanket of white killing of hope of a half marathon in Stowmarket. However, the following weekend the snowfall cleared for Colchester. England's oldest recorded dwelling, once the capital of Roman Britain they called Camulodium, the mile, a measurement the Latins introduced.

Veteran soldiers from the empire retired there, and so too a few players from Ipswich Town Football Club. The most famed gladiator, Kevin Beattie. Lest we forget Jungle Boy Ray Crawford, part of the renowned giant killing team, taking Mighty Leeds to the sword, young and old, running on the turf in celebration. David and Goliath tales told father to son wrapped in gold with a pinch of nostalgia, reposted in prose for modern ages.

Legends now celebrated in stone, the bowed effigies misunderstood, Kings and Queens Kill and lame, no mortal a God or Goddess. Statues dotted on every corner of this Isle, some deserved and other bought, we speak of true heroics in wistful tones, sat fireside on winter days. The Beat, The King, Bestie, Coe, Ovett, Oxford's miler and all the wonderful people I have met.

Colchester United, my son and I adopted as a second team when he was small, and on occasions, we travelled the short drive, the modern stadium and ours 18 miles apart. The metallic structure resembles a giant spaceship just touched down on earth, and in a poetic twist, a frozen burger sent it into space attached to a weather balloon recently landed there.

The annual half marathon starts and finish outside the football ground. March 18th, I saw a few familiar faces and jumped over the railings into a swift corral. Stood amongst a cast of thousands, adrenaline rose to ignite hope. Gun fired, cheers from crowd the moment I strode forward, I noticed the top of my thigh tight, after leaping the barrier.

The first bit of the course downhill, North Hill sapped the energy on route through the undulating town. Essex not so flat I grabbed a drink passing the Norman Castle resting on the foundations of a Roman Villa burnt a cinder by Boudicca the flame haired warrior Queen. The city rose again, with a wall to protect that survives today, as if modern streets a temporary blip lying over a melting pot of history.

Up for the fight, the thigh tight, I kept under eight minute pace, and with a Swiss conversion at 10k I swallowed a gel counting to 100 running fast and then another easy, the brain the critical organ in mastering the body's destiny. Pain information, dulled in endorphins, ignored at your peril, albeit embraced in victory.

During the run, many potholes scarred the highways. Marshalls calling out to warn of hazards ahead, I thought it poetic Romans roads survived under the crumbling tarmac. Halfway, leaving the town crossing the A12 into Langham, high trees framing the course, we could have been anywhere in England.

People handed out Jelly babies outside the pub and the terrain flattened, I gained back time, digging deep, pace held counting white lines and potted holes. A runner behind, personal trainer in tow, off-putting, I became an unwilling pacer. The veteran gave his all, his fitness guru several metres ahead, running backwards and shouting encouragement.

Parkrun to go, tactics tipped from the window ledge. Survival a must with trees blocking Constables Country view, I ran through the scene of the Battle of Boxted Heath, where ordinary people and forces of royal fought each other for control of England. Humpty Dumpty a childhood rhyme is perhaps the Royalist cannon that fell from Roman Colchester's walls, sowing a sea of charge in which democracy remains, shell unbroken.

On the home straight, teeth gritted, eyes narrow, looking for the stadium, the heart almost surrendered. As I approached Stadio supreme, the sound of the PA and crowd a lift, I swung left, the finish line appearing for a decisive effort. One hour and forty-five minutes of toil, the target achieved one's body relieved.

Afterwards, recovered, sipping a coke in fresh clothes stood centre stage on the pitch, I saw an old friend. Twiggy half a man he used to be was once an acrobatic goalkeeper. Now both runners, passaging time seamless, I took a shot at goal he saved with a customary roll.

Impressed with the event, my red carpet was a shortcut across waste ground to the carpark with a footballing pal from yesteryear. For who was Stan but several people, I knew, forever young. Life not wasted on youth, every story encompasses a start, middle and end curved in experience, born from naïveté.

I have much to learn and see. You only live twice, part two, a wiser journey stripped of vanity with joyful memories to rewind and pass on to those who care to listen, not wanting to tread a tumbling path lost in a maze.

Today I do not require a map of life, although driving to the race a fool such as I missed a turn with stadium insight and headed hence forth to Chelmsford on a road to nowhere. Warm up neglected, no winner's trophy kissed, but a memory and tale to tell, destiny mine.

Time to open one's ears to new ideas, I see two suitcases, one shiny, a younger you, the other full of junk. Would you want an empty case or another bursting with memories to embrace? I choose the latter, destination 50, a journey, the backpack overflowing with seeds to sow, beer in Ramsholt Arms gazing out upon the River Deben.

Three cities one heart

Mile 25

'Creator of life, are you there, I have words I wish to share?'

Mark Lankester

Deep in thought, I stare out into the garden and spot a parakeet. I have read that Jimi Hendrix once freed a pair in Carnaby Street, for the birds we see today are their ancestors. An unlikely tale I yearn to believe, although learned folk think me naïve.

Urban myths did I trust in childhood innocence. Science debunks and chapter 25 the finish in sight, I wanted to give up the fight. Yet, the right fraction of the brain lit a fire within, and now imagination fuelled let us begin...

Creation is hard when locked in survival, for how do you write, stuck in a rat race that sucks the head of ideas, the ink depleted. Dreams maketh man, so I keep the faith. We are mere visitors in this world, and why waste a precious gift. Life is no dress rehearsal, and our legacy is the energy we pass on to others.

Imagine a utopia of rolling hills, sun kissed beaches and blue skies, where nobody struggled and no babies cried through hunger. Withal, raising a wall to protect a nirvana from those wishing to share is itself a prison and as I stride out on country trails, I cannot comprehend a nation shut in concrete suppression.

The butterfly fragile and free, a symbol of transformation and joy I no longer believe in famed stars and statues of gold, and have hope in the millennials optic vision untarnished by a strawberry field.

Living on an island looking for another line, midlife stripped my drive to shake the status quo, and I surf the waves of sensibility, swerving ominous menace. Yet, I dread falling from the board beneath the tide, my only weapon a senseless rhyme, fitness a shelter and veil.

Inspired, I had never raced abroad unless you count Edinburgh, city of statues, the heavens a wide-open door where God's tears swirl and pour. A B&B in Leith, Easter Road, on the doorstep of the Holy Ground, stood a beacon of faith. The club's colours a historic clue, to remind of the Isle of Hibernia. Home a rustic rural landscape familiar, I felt one had roamed those streets in another life.

Saint Patrick, a Romantic Briton enslaved in Ireland, spread the word of God. Question to ponder, are we our place of birth, or a product of our ancestors. Gothic childhood tales feared no more: a wind of change whistles in one's lungs, as the skin reddens and fades with every season.

Edinburgh's festival of running a wet affair, I trudged the roads of Auld Reekie. Pre-race as I sheltered from the deluge, I found a poor soul asleep under sodden blankets. Dickensian stories ring true in modern Britain. For daily, we passed a homeless man on a bench outside the Palace of Holyroodhouse, residence of the Queen.

Whilst surrounded by thousands of souls, dozens of sculptures dotted the landscape as we weaved out of Scottish Inventions. The ploughman poet Robert Burns for one, shining through dampened skies, influenced by Greeks of Athens with its plinth greened bronze. Rob said hope springs on a triumphant wing, and Auld Lang Syne is a song I sing.

The finish line in coastal Musselburgh, its ocean waves smashed along the promenade walls, striking my sodden face, adding a salt tang. Never had I craved a run so much to end, and even though smiling faces handed out sweets and cheered, it was the pain I feared.

Post-race, we discovered a pub that served Suffolk ale and I got talking to a local who lamented George Best who plied his trade for a year in the hoops of Hibernian. I could have reminisced longer, but after a single pint we left, one's better half having suffered the elements spectating, more deserving of a medal than I.

Reading the works of author Italo Calvino was of far more interest than busting a lung, searching for the non-existent Knight. Edinburgh's Marathon Festival started in the city and ended up nine miles away in

Pinkie Fields. A long walk and bus ride back to base, misted windows and no carnival to embrace.

Sun cream not required and windswept and fed wandering Leith to find our pad we trod the path of Oliver's Army. An abode of artisan class, longing for the warmth of a gas fire, I could see Salisbury Crags and the football ground that so inspired.

Stratus clouds did light up the night, and it was hard to sleep. So I listened to the news and feared Ipswich Town's fate, sad to watch the game they play, our legends soon forgotten, and the rudderless ship's hull nigh on rotten. People paint faces and no stars shine without mortal witness, for they fill the canvas with a timbre of richness.

The day after the race, we awoke early to climb the hill we saw from our kitchen. Arthur's Seat, Robert Louis Stevenson, described as a mountain of virtue. Slippery rocks beneath a watery sky, summit conquered, we gazed out on the horizon, Hibs stadio supreme gleaming green as if a tiny emerald.

The stroll downward we discovered St Margaret's Loch, the resident swans, mallards and great crested grebes a delight to watch. J. K Rowley wrote gothic wizard tales within the rustic cafes, and a raven I saw perched upon a pole guarding the Stone of Destiny.

On a volcanic crag stands a castle, Lothian's historic fortress. Not lofty as the seat of Arthur and not cheap to enter, we returned whence we came strolling the Royal mile admiring the classical buildings. Echoes bagpipes and so many choices I heard the cry of distant voices.

Fuelled with caffeine, the sights and sounds beguiled, trekking the capital of Caledonia. In youth on wet winter days, I smoked, puffing along heart filled with a metallic beat. That was my world. Today heaven is living, and I ask for no more.

Edinburgh rivals Rome in culture both built on seven hills. Scholars grew from this land woven with poetic prose, and one of many was romanticist Walter Scott, author of Ivanhoe and Rob Roy. The monument tower that celebrates his influence, gothic in style, stands 200 feet high, a steep climb that sweeps the eye with a cloud Atlas.

Home of Romans our next port of call, a country within a city the Mediterranean troops once walked the streets of Scotland, and a misunderstood wall builds a false window into history. The Colosseum and Trevi Fountain shining in triumph, I ventured out jogging in the midday sol.

Memories fade but old injuries linger, the air thin and lungs burning, I was in a hurry to get a tan and embrace Italia's seat of learning. Apprendimento velocemente pace could not last, body wilting outside Hostaria Glass in a tale of time and repercussion.

Christianity brought from Roma to Britannia did a saint take to the Emerald Isle; its ancestors forming Hibs on Easter Road onward to the Vatican we strode. Lost within Giardini Vaticani mobile signal dead, I gazed at a cross, and then knew where the path led.

Too beautiful to race, Italy at a different pace, pizza, and ice cream as the sun did shimmer, captivated in the land of Vespa by a mod revelation. A candle lit and a pray in the Pantheon rebuilt by Hadrian, Corinthian columns, and a marble hall, a beam of light from the dome up high, a ruined forum and Capitoline hills I marvelled at the architectural skills, Piazza Novena, and Spanish steps we sat admiring Bernini sculptures.

Once upon a time in Berlin, John Kennedy ordered a jelly donut. God loves a trier. The only rhyme that bites is a word written that declares its meaning. Rebirth, a life awoken armed with wisdom ready to roll, a book of prose to learn. Plan, order a beer fluent in German, and run a half marathon, neither easy.

The Big Five-O, a milestone to celebrate, birthday nigh, I was to endeth this tale, finish line a mile, internet names of cities to fly, the Pope Revenge catching the eye. Born Easter Sunday, a day of rest, I intended to wear my vest, Felixstowe emblazoned in red, in a capital raised from ashes fought and bled.

The night before the flight, having relived much the brain spinning with ideas, I dreamt an unsettling vibrant tale. I am walking in woodland, the forest silent, and march on forth spotting a distant light. Friend or foe, it did not matter, and in a scene of black and white, shots rang out a deafening cry. For it was not my dream, but an echo of history and childhood tales.

Saturday, April 6th, 2018 awoken at 2am, the build-up a concern I arrived at the Expo held at the former

Tempelhof Airport with a handful of German phrases; muddled in voice. Well, I gave it a go, and she smiled and said 'hello'.

Once in our hotel in Karl Marx Allee we crashed out exhausted, stirring to the hum of traffic. Our intention was to have breakfast at the race that started and finished a short stroll from where we stayed. Poor in prep, but confident I could get round in reasonable shape, we found a stall that sold bagels.

April 7th with 36,000 souls, running Berlin in glorious sunshine, I paid the price. Approaching the Brandenburg Gate just inside the old east side, fatigued with heavy legs, Garmin died the second I passed under the imposing monument.

The iconic symbol now a sign of unity instead of division, I have seen the landmark on television battled and scarred and as I ran, memorials shadowed the city, the sight of Oberbaun Bridge so pretty.

Checkpoint Charlie stood next to Ronald McDonald, an unintentional irony noted when finished, supping non-alcoholic Erdinger lager. High on the atmosphere, I discovered the bar beer real, and adrenaline fuelled I met a celeb. Name forgotten and comedy his fame; I mentioned I was from Ipswich. Sutton Hoo midlife run, he plans to retire in Woodbridge, a joker's son.

The event experienced as a runner and spectator, folk smiled, runners danced, and a few struggled in visible distress. I saw an older man, determined not to walk, and felt his pain. Yet heart skipping a beat his grandson took his hand, tears of joy sweeping his face, on they marched full of grace.

Day two, we joined with English-speaking sightseers and an Australian guide. A Kiwi named Noah an eccentric, amongst Scots, Irish, and a commonwealth of nations. A historic tour de force, we strode on admiring present and past Alexanderplatz and grey stone flats, graffiti coloured and worn, Victory Column and the Reichstag reborn.

The capital today prospers full of diversity with The Fernsehturm, a true buster of clouds, dominating the skyline. Built in 1969, a restaurant rotates within the retro si-fi tower so visitors can view the metropolis. Popes Revenge is the name given by locals, because when the sun shines on the steel dome, a cross reflects. Christs sign, that frightened, and inspired in equal measure a comfort to the suppressed, now rises for a unified country. Pleased to say, the reflection shone throughout our stay.

'Tis not my place to write of war, for historians are better qualified. Therefore, I speak of the vibe of a city. Howbeit, it is impossible to ignore salient facts.

No-man's-land is today the site of a holocaust memorial surrounded by shops, cafes and businesses. Large stone slabs- 2711 in a total stand in symmetrical rows on an uneven surface, creating a maze, and when we were on lower ground, they towered over us, the experience profound and moving.

David Bowie sang of heroes when he played an open-air gig in West Berlin, music flowing as if a butterfly with a message to young and old in the east throughout the night's sky, prompting many to rush the wall and chant in lyrical defiance.

The Thin White Duke's song of lovers segregated by the barricade became Berliner's personal anthem. When he died, so inspirational his power to move individuals, the German Foreign Office posted a tweet on social media to thank him.

We spent the last day of our tour at Friedrichshain Park, where earth-covered debris has now matured into two hilltops. People of divergent origins and age sat making barbecues, drinking and playing music. Sunset arrived, and we noted many runners careening the pathways, running a global speech.

One touching story of millions struck an intimate arc, when I learnt that the last person shot at the wall was a lad of 20. In 2018, he should have praised his 50th birthday, but tragically, a humble tribute dedicated to him rests on the bank of the city's canal. Freedom a luxury I took for granted, his bravery wholehearted, I know not what path I would have chosen.

I want to be high and pain-free running forever through stratus clouds, easy on a Sunday morning with cousins gazing out on to the Rhine with a differing voice making the same choice. Gerry my pacemaker, far from home, mortal bone Saxon fields I roam.

Beware of ignorance beguiled, dragging you from your life in their name, for they want fame your souls theirs to waste on a whim. For I reap the reward of my forebears, crushed and broken, their pain unspoken. Ode to joy, Europe's anthem a tune to sing in any voice, freedom is something to rejoice.

April 14th, I celebrated half a century reborn. An individual artist lost in an orchestra with a conductor telling me how to play, Berlin shone bright and true, showing the way. Love is the word, and if you believe that, you will walk through a storm with your head held high in triumph.

God is in the world we live, his answer not his to give, we find truth in the air that we breathe. Druid the Celtic term for oak, the tree stretches out towards heaven rooted in earthly ground. A man of contradiction, I never go to church and speak of religion. Yet, I carry St Christopher whence I travel hidden from view. Fired and inspired, we tread.

The beginning

Mile 26

'Get back up, enjoy and embrace, for tomorrow is
another race.'

Mark Lankester

An oak tree lives generations and bears witness to
change. An acorn, a sapling and later teenage leaves,
its arms frame the stars. For we are, part of something
continuous and the longer one lingers, the deeper the
roots weave entwined with earth. A father with a tone
as local as fields, I belong nowhere else.

Fate can take a fickle path sailing forth, despite the
best of intentions. Albeit, in a cyclone of change,
sometimes we discover a brighter Isle and see the
world through a differing eye, with a guiding light
followed.

If living were a movie edited to our pleasure, we
would stare ahead with a wide causeway, a simple
stroll to our dreams not foreseeing an unscripted
flood, a rocky climb a gale and a director that shouts
cut, with a different take, demanding a coffee break.

The manner we Suffolk folk talk we hail a humdrum
task, a bit of rigmarole, and an anomaly a right
rumun. On the drag supping a cup of three, I never

speak the ol' mawthers Queens English. Oh joy, imagine if I had written this book the way one muttered, strewth, the consternation.

Now well past 50 a fresh decade approaching I slip on the green of Kesgrave Kruisers, a newborn running club, the kit an emerald clue, as I jog the lanes of Rushmere, Martlesham and Foxhall older in body but sharper mind with a belief in destiny.

Yesterday I discovered a poem scribbled in childhood. Ipswich ruled Europe, Elvis was King, and I knew not what life would bring, but the nation of the free beguiled. Hundreds of years ago, Pilgrim Fathers sailed forth to a new world. A hufen grut way with a hope and a pray, on arrival they planted Suffolk towns on America's east coast. Generations later, a few returned, masters of the skies in echoed voice, and for that, we rejoice.

Once on a school trip, as children played, I paused, examining a muddy trail. Miss, a young schoolteacher, did not yell, and I pointed out that a puddle beneath my feet resembled Australia. Curious, she asked if I liked geography as I marked countries in the soil with a twig, and although embarrassed in her presence, there were no walls to clip thy wings.

Fireside fables of gladiators of old The Beat scored from a mile, his heading legendary in a team of style. Framlingham bound Ed wrote of a Castle on a hill, genius farmers invent and council estates spawn poets; we an understated tribe. God's country without hills, Constable and Gainsborough painted the scene, and Robson and Ramsey gave us the dream.

January 25th, 2019, the writing done, brain weary, it was time to go run. Lost in a land the mind distracted, the limbs stiff and fingers numb passing the Kesgrave Bell, I prayed for divine intervention. Home and 17 miles covered on ice-coated roads, I had much to accomplish.

Days and weeks followed, and I ventured through Christchurch Park and said hello to Mabel plodding the paths of Kings and Queens, and the sculpture of the forgotten. Two more long runs and a valentine pursuit through Rushmere, Garmin recorded the tale.

Spring arrived, and summer near I hit the trails of Brookhill Wood and saw a fox and a deer. May, shin splints, Colchester 10k and no chip timing, flaming June I sought a Saxon village and with an outline of Great Britain drawn on Strava on the 25th, flying high confidence grew.

August 20th 7pm on a balmy summer's evening in Kesgrave I stood on the field fit to roll surrounded by 40 souls with a novel unshared. For, having joined the warm-up decades too late, life had spun full circle.

The left calf sore despite half a tube of Ibuprofen gel, I tried touching my toes, and struggled with the simplest of manoeuvres. I felt my age surprised how easy fellow athletes made the task look, my Benfleet 15 tee shirt a badge of honour, as if to say I was once a runner.

The session that night was fartlek, sharp bursts of speed followed by recovery. Happy the book concluded I was back, adrenaline pumping. Howbeit, on listening to instruction, the brain denied the request to rest between efforts, and I sped on round the cricket pitch chasing those fleet of foot.

The first mile swift, I wondered if I could achieve an unofficial PB for 5 miles. The last two in 7:06 and 7:04 with screaming calves, I sensed I had scaled a sierra and teetered far afield to collect one's thoughts. Five-minute shy of my fastest, it was foolish, but the fact I attempted the feat was a note of confidence.

A Raging Bull has no strategy, its power surges uncontrolled. For the film noir movie of the same name, a depressing watch, one scene I found an inspiration. Beaten and still standing, a defeat is victory if not crushed. For although LaMotta lost his crown, Sugar Ray never knocked him canvas bound.

I have a big race planned this year; The Great East Run. Ipswich Town's beloved half marathon on September the 22nd, takes in the splendour of the Orwell Bridge, the waterfront and the glorious Suffolk countryside. The finish at the football ground, a fitting conclusion. Withal, a new beginning, tomorrow a new life, the throbbing leg proof of distance travelled.

Fingers crossed, I have purchased a foam roller to help appease the pain. Freston Hill is a demanding section of the course, and I have just been to investigate. Monkey Lodge on the summit overlooks the River Orwell, once a lookout for Smugglers. Ape in the window a sign of safe passage, childhood tales embellished, I know not the truth.

Seventy thousands words my greatest deed achieved, I hope you enjoy these pages when I find the courage to share. Thwart those demons and thrive. Plans for the future: an Ultra Marathon in 2022, I desire, with a wondrous world to probe, and a heart filled with joy.

Goodbye for now, the story is just beginning, reborn, lines on face a map, the eyes a guide. What we learn on route eclipses bewilderment of youth, and if you judge this a pontification, you take a walk along our waterfront to witness the celebration. A nod and a wink I spy a pal and smile without a word spoken, for we have walked these streets in another life.

Hope

385 yards

' We keep the finish line out of reach, the sea washing over the sand one wave at a time, a grain so small we circle and return whence we came.'

Mark Lankester

The last steps of the London marathon were a moment, its brevity sublime. I continue to rhyme, for what we understand with a verse says so much more. See their race, but never know what lurks beneath those eyes. Understanding a poem is an enigma, its code locked within the writer's brain, the right sphere worn.

Fifty thousand steps, toes raw on Roman roads, was a Greek distance I quashed a saddened grin. The start and completion of a contrasting tale, one man's pain is another's majesty. For I pen a text about life, a trail every mortal has taken.

Mature enough to vote, one's frontal lobe undeveloped, wisdom a slow burn yet to flame. Mistakes and missteps mark a route warned, walkable in maturity. Vitality is belief, and a quadrophonic symphony of who am I. Adulthood, a trophy won once teenage kicks sour, tainted in middle age, today maturity is a friend, and faith a compass.

Beowulf a poet, I read muddled words unearthed, the finish gantry shining, and the palace gates gold and within sight. Queen Boadicea on one's shoulder, Britannica bronzed and relived, United Kingdom flags a flutter, I peer at my timepiece breathless, days of lore puffs of vapour.

The race did endeth recessional, but with a stew of a word and voice yet heard, I continue to write. Turn a page and sure to age, our bodies a gift if the brain doth listen. A grey matter so misunderstood, our potential is power, and truth a moonlit path that lights the   flame.

Don't miss out!

Click the button below and you can sign up to receive emails whenever Mark Lankester publishes a new book. There's no charge and no obligation.

https://books2read.com/r/B-A-FJVN-TOANB

BOOKS 2 READ

Connecting independent readers to independent writers.

About the Author

Mark is a keen runner who has run the streets and trails of his home in Ipswich, Suffolk in England for 25 years. Today a familiar face in the green of running club Kesgrave Kruisers.

Printed in Great Britain
by Amazon